Stay S...

Football, Banking, Scouting and Me;

THE JOURNEY

BY JOHN STARRS

To Peter

Good Luck & Best Wishes

John S.

ISBN   978-1-907516-47-4

Design © **TUCANNLtd**

Produced by: **TUCANNLtd**

Unit 9 Blackthorn Way | Five Mile Business Park | Washingborough | Lincoln LN4 1BF

t: 01522 790009 | e: studio@tucann.co.uk | w: tucann.co.uk

KEVIN AUSTIN
(12.02.1973 – 23.11.2018)

© *Scunthorpe United*

I would like to dedicate these memories to Kevin Austin. I never met him, I never spoke to him, but he changed my life when I watched him play and recommended him to Fulham FC in 1998. He got me into scouting. He never knew it and I will be forever grateful; I only wish I could have met him to say thank you in person.

He struck me as a player with a great physical presence who was equally strong on the ball as well as off the ball. After all this time one thing still stands out about his performance. I recall him shielding the ball from an opponent on the corner of the 18-yard box all the way back to his own goal line before letting the ball run out for a goal kick, an amazing show of strength.

I've had a wonderful experience meeting great people and having much success, all down to Kevin Austin. Thank you from me, and it was a great shock to learn of his death at the age of just 45.

Rest in Peace Kevin Austin

ACKNOWLEDGMENTS

I must address the guys who put the idea in my head in the first place (Pierre Quinquenel & Andy Francis). I received an Email from Pierre asking me if I would be interested in playing a football match along with others from the 1970s whom I played with for NatWest Bank. This was an annual event, but as most are of a similar age or older than me (age 66), the people available to play is diminishing year by year. I politely declined, and replied as follows…

Hi All,

I would love to be able to play but as my wife Lynda says I have trouble walking up the garden now never mind playing football, due to a heart condition and the onset of early stages of Parkinson's. So, it's a polite decline from me I am afraid.

For those around that may remember me, I joined NatWest Bank in August 1970, and started playing later that year. I was around until 1978 when I returned to Doncaster.

I played for the first team and reserves, as well as Hyde Park Area and the regional side when I was not injured.

I played with players such as Ted Taylor, Bert Lean, Howie Bristow, Dave Collard, Alan Webb, Paul

Williams, Jim McLay, Alan Cook (I was the only one to ever get him booked in an area game) to name but a few I hope your day goes well on the day, I will be thinking of you all on the day. Apologies to any one whose name I have not mentioned.

All the best to all, and especially those who I played with. I remember my time at NORBURY with fondness, and perhaps the amount of lager and Bacardi I consumed with my teammates after games eventually has caught me up.

Best wishes again to all,

John Starrs

Several discussions later, following various emails where I mentioned my involvement in scouting, this is the end result.

A big thank you to both of you who made me believe I had a story in there somewhere.

Next, I must address Kit and Tom from TUCANNdesign&print for their time, help, support and all-round involvement (most importantly the publishing part).

Ironically, the first time I went around to put my idea to them, I met Kit who was wearing a M********* United top. I warned him straight away that he wouldn't like me, but after five minutes I'd decided that I wanted to pursue this book with them. I'm a big believer in things that are meant to be, and the fact he also has a cricket top with NatWest as the sponsors on strengthened that.

Furthermore, when I met his grandfather Tom, I was impressed with the way he left me in no doubt I was with the right people after talking to me about how to market my book. As you're reading this part now, I can't have done a bad job marketing it, so I thank you for giving me the confidence to do that.

It's funny to think in that first meeting, I handed Kit my book (around 40-50 A4 pages) which I thought was close to being finished.

How wrong was I?

Since that first meeting, the book has grown and grown just from little ideas he has given me into what you're holding in your hands right now.

I couldn't have done it without you!

Thank you.

Paul, Karla & Lynda

The next part is to Lynda, my long-suffering wife. You have been there through most of the actual experiences and have heard all the stories time after time after time over the years. So, to put you through them all again while putting this book together. Thank you!

The next bit is to my son, Paul, and his girlfriend, Karla. They both work in the gambling trade, in Gibraltar, for respective companies, William Hill & Coral. Paul is an Imp through and through. So much so, that sometimes he flies all the way home to come and watch them play! Karla on the other hand supports Liverpool. This year has obviously been excellent for banter with it being such a close finish between our respective sides. I'm just glad we finished ahead of them because I'm not sure how I'd have coped otherwise.

I can't not say a big thank you to Kevin Keegan for giving me the opportunity in scouting in the first place, but also our friendship over the years. He has been of great support in helping with ideas to be imputed into the final book and I thank him for agreeing to do the foreword for my book.

ALLAN WEBB (WEBBY)
(24.07.1947 – 29.03.2019)

Allan Webb Team & Allan Webb in his younger years.

Whilst writing these memories I was informed that Allan was very seriously ill and has since passed away. I played with Allan back in the 1970s for NatWest Bank.

With my professional scouting hat on now that I have worked as a senior Scout for Manchester City first team for 19 years, I would say this about Allan (Webby) as a player looking back.

Allan was National Westminster Bank's answer to Bobby Moore. He had class on and off the ball, he never looked flustered always seemed to be in control, whilst not the quickest he had great positional sense. He would have been comfortable as an all-round defender or even as they say these days, a number 6 (holding player).

He was probably one of the best defenders I ever played with. He could have played I have no doubt at a higher level and got paid for his efforts.

As I played in front of him sometimes as a winger, he kept me focused and you dare not make a mistake or he let you know. He had high standards, a very cultured player.

Allan loved all sports, but Football was his first choice. He never lost his love for the game; if he was not watching Sky Sports, he was listening to TalkSport.

Crystal Palace and his Dad's team Arsenal were the teams he supported, so I don't know what he would have thought of me scouting for Fulham, never mind Manchester City, but I have it on good authority from his wife, Jan, that he would've been proud of me.

Rest in peace Allan

CONTENTS

FOREWORD BY KEVIN KEEGAN

I have known John (Starrzy) for almost sixty years when we were in our early teens, we both played for the St Peters football team in Doncaster, Yorkshire. John was a very similar player to me, we were both wingers, both pretty quick and we both didn't lack courage. The only major difference was that Starrzy had a wonderful left foot and I didn't.

When I joined Fulham, I asked John about a player who was from his area and he gave me an assessment that was so close to my top scout's report that I decided to ask him to do some work for me and watch another player we had been keeping an eye on for some time. The report came back, and it was so accurate and well-presented that I then asked him if he would like to become more involved with us at Fulham F.C.

Since then of course he has managed to stand the test of time as a scout and had the ability to stay involved with big clubs in a fast and ever-changing working environment.

His book should inspire other people to realise that there are many ways to be involved in the great game of football – John stumbled in to scouting but found his feet very quickly and of course I am very proud to say that my friend Starrzy the scout made it to the very top of the game. KK

1

WHO STARTED THE BALL ROLLING?

For many years now friends have told me to write down the stories that follow, with them saying, "You must have some stories to tell." This also applies to complete strangers that I have met on holiday. Recently on a cruise around the Spanish coast and especially a small hotel in Scotland, everyone got a different story or two and they all told me the same thing, "You must write these down!"

It usually starts over a beer at the bar or breakfast, when you start to talk to people who are on holiday.

Eventually the conversation turns around to, "So, what do you do for a living?" Well I used to say I am (or was) a Regional Bank Manager.

Work at the bank day job was so stressful. My son Paul and Lynda, unbeknown to me booked me a week away on a Greek island called Kalymnos, on my own. It was very strange, especially the first few days. However as usual I got talking to various people just casually especially a young couple whom I had met on the first day. They asked me what I did I told them about my banking job and skimmed over it.

However, the next day I was by the pool on a sunbed with them on one side and an old boy who was on a bed relaxing on the other with me in between. I remember them saying to me, "It must be stressful your job giving financial advice which could affect people's lives." I responded, "Yes it can be", and we left it at that.

However, within about 10 minutes the old boy, plucked up the courage to say, "I could not help overhearing that you are a financial

Bank Manager. I, of course, said yes that's right. He then went into overdrive telling me his financial situation and asking for advice! After about 30 minutes where I covered in very general terms his financial situation, without being precise, such as you must not have all your eggs in one basket, you should aim for a balanced portfolio be aware of the various risk strategies in what you're investing in, and don't forget the golden rule. If it sounds too good to be true, then it probably is. He concluded, "That's been very useful. You have given me confidence that I am on the right track."

I had told him nothing really that he did not already know, but he went away happy to the bar. The young couple turned to me and said you were great with him, it must have been the last thing you needed or wanted to discuss, I replied, "Yes, in fact it was what I was trying to get away from." From that day, I decided to park the Bank Manager role when people ask me what I do. Instead, I just mention football.

From that over the years people now ask me, "So who have you discovered?" This starts the conversation on to other football related stories such as, "How did you get involved in Scouting?" When I tell them, this opens up avenues for other questions, usually finishing with me telling them a few stories that you will find in the contents of this book. You should write these stories down they often say. So here we are twenty-one years or so later, with many stories to tell.

When I look at both careers, I can see parallels in that the study of body language is important in both. One, being decisive and the other, not sitting on the fence.

Banking requires you to be confident in front of customers in that you know what you are doing, that you can use your observational skills to back up your comment with a fact, being disciplined in the way one tackles problems and much more. You must remember you won't get it right every time. For example, every bank manager worth his salt will lose money somewhere, every scout will get a player recommendation wrong sooner or later but both situations can be explained if the evidence is there to back up your reason for coming to that conclusion.

I would add that when I was trying to make it as a professional player, failure meant that it was effectively the end of the dream, that is not the case anymore, there are so many doors that open when another door closes now, whilst I had a background in football which without doubt helped me analyse both players and team performance, what is certain now is that the days of the old style scout who came into the role when their career as a player was over are now on the way to extinction. I know of very experienced scouts who retired because they could not adapt to the new technical way reports had to be submitted, via computer. They had not lost the ability to assess a player or a team, but they had not moved on with the times.

The scouting role is now in the hands of young guys. Mainly university graduates who are technically minded, who can operate a computer and analyse data. When you watch a game now on Sky etc., statistics are at the front of everything you see such as: possession, shots on target, distance covered by each player, shots off target, and that breakdown of information is growing by the day. Even adapting information for match reports, to show things in a different manner to assist the Manager in his preparation for the up and coming fixture.

I hope in some way the contents of this book will show people out there that they can get involved in some way from the various roles now available in the professional game other than as a player.

I would also say first and foremost, that anyone picking up this book enjoys the whole experience and will try to be a scout for the day by assessing a player when watching a game either live or on the television, picking out your man of the match and analysing his match for fun to see if the so called experts agree with you. It may just give you the confidence over time to pick up that phone or write to your local club and give a recommendation, you never know, as my son once said to me, "Dad, if you don't ask the question, the answers always going to be NO!"

It is without doubt, a fun and rewarding job. I would add that once you think like a scout, you will never watch a game again in the same way; you will always analyse.

I hope you enjoy football in a different way from now on and the information about what a scout needs to look for will be of assistance in prolonging the life of the old-style scout for many years to come.

This includes the ladies out there as well because there are many out there who believe that Lynda is the real scout in the family. John Ferguson for one, and Gavin Fleig as well. In their company, she has not been short to voice her opinion on a player. You may think I am joking, but I trust her judgement without question. If there was a mark that went lower than "D" such as an "E", she would give it more often than I would.

2

FOOTBALL DECIDED I SHOULD JOIN A BANK

As I always said on bank courses that I've attended. I either wanted to play football or join a bank. Football, or more to the point Lawrie McMenemy (Manager of Doncaster Rovers at the time 1970) decided, I should join a bank.

I recall back in the summer of 1970, I was in pre-season training at Doncaster Rovers, at that time the youth players like me age 17 and younger used to have to do things like clean the senior pro's boots and do some of the maintenance of the stadium, at that time it was at Belle View across from the race course.

It was a very hot summer and one job I remember doing with others was to get the stadium ready for the new season by what was known as snowceming the white wall around the perimeter of the pitch, it was a horrible job.

I also remember a young player like myself called Alan Machin who was a character but a very good player much better than me, he used to get up to all sorts of mischief.

I remember one morning the youth players including myself were sat in the home dressing room waiting for the boss (Lawrie McM) to come and give us our jobs for the day after training, he came in with a stern look on his face and said "ok who was it? Who was the smart a***."

We all sat there looking vacant the boss asked again, then one more time but adding if you don't own up you will all get extra training, and it was a blistering hot day, so now we all looked at each other.

Suddenly, Alan put his hand up admitting "it was me boss." Lawrie McM told us all to leave the room while he spoke to Alan.

It turned out that as usual local business used to drop off the occasional gift for the Manager, and the day before the local shop keeper had delivered a full tray of 24 free range eggs. Alan, had got hold of these while we were all coming back in from training and promptly hard boiled every single egg putting them back on the tray which the gaffer took home to his wife.

When she tried to crack open one of the eggs, well you can guess her reaction. The boss was not amused, but I think he did see the funny side of the prank at his expense. Alan was what you would call a Gazza of his day always doing something.

Another player I must mention who was a legend playing for Doncaster is Alick Jeffrey (29th January 1939- 22nd November 2000 - Age 61).

Who? I hear you ask.

He made his debut for Doncaster Rovers at the age of 15. He quickly became known as the 'The Boy Wonder', destined for bigger and better things however, fate played a cruel part in his career and I implore you to read about his bad luck and what could have been.

When he came on the scene, aged 15, the famous Manchester United assistant manager, Jimmy Murphy labelled him the "English Pele" – yes, he was that good!

In the latter part of his career, he was playing for Doncaster Rovers, whom I used to go and watch week in, week out. He was very overweight and had no real pace, but he still more often than not, was the best player on the pitch every week by a country mile. He would definitely be taking the man of the match award home every week.

Before he was transferred to Lincoln City, I had the privilege to be on the same training pitch as him. We were doing laps at Sandal Beat, which is adjacent to the Racecourse Ground. To begin with, Alick was ahead of the rest of us, but that soon changed. On lap two, he had been overtaken by most of us and after the third lap, he was bent over gasping for breath. The next bit I remember to this day, Lawrie McM turned to him and sent him inside. He was transferred to Lincoln shortly afterwards. It may have only been brief but I will always remember the training session I had with the 'English Pele'.

The legacy of him is the Alick Jeffrey Way (the road around the Doncaster stadium) and then one of the five apartment blocks situated where Belle Vue used to be have been named after him.

Unfortunately for me, after I had finished snowceming the wall around the pitch, I was called into the office and released also. I still think about the fact that they waited until the wall was clean and sparkling before telling me my time at Doncaster Rovers had come to an end. Not so long afterwards, I joined National Westminster Bank in London, and started work at Lower Sloane Street branch which was on the edge of the Kings Road.

I left for London and joined NatWest on the 10th August 1970, with my hopes of a football career over, or so I thought. When you joined the Bank in those days, you had to complete a six-month probation before you were confirmed, or not as a full-time employee. To be fair, they were so short of staff you would have had to be a total numpty/ idiot not to pass the probation period

I recall I had very little time from my first interview to actually starting work. My mother arranged for me to stay with some long-term friends of hers called Mr and Mrs Bow. They lived in Kilburn,

North London, on Abbey Road near the famous Zebra crossing with their daughter Cecilia (as far as I can remember). I was working in the Kings Road and now living in the well-known, thanks to the Beatles, Abbey Road.

My father owned the only suit in the house, and I needed to wear one for work in the Bank. So, I took the suit and went to London leaving him suit-less. I was introduced to the neighbours by Mr & Mrs Bow, one of which was a tailor who offered to make me a suit, which I agreed at cost price as I had very little money. It turned out, to my surprise, that the tailor worked in Saville Row. I was now the proud owner of my first suit from the most prestigious area for tailoring in the world, not a bad start.

Strangely enough, a few years ago Manchester City got all the scouts measured for club suits. They were being ordered from John Lewis in Manchester. However, when my suit arrived, for some reason it came from Alexanders of Savile Row!! Spooky or what?

In that previous 3 months, I had not gone anywhere near a football, I had taken the fact that I was not going to be a professional harder than I thought and was not really interested.

However, around the same time my father rang me to say it's up to you, but he gave me his opinion, Dunfermline Athletic have been on the phone and want you to go to Scotland for a month's trial.

This would mean I would have to resign from NatWest and take the chance that I would get a contract with Dunfermline. My world was turned upside down, I had been given one more chance, what should I do!!??

I thought it over for 24 hours and decided that it was a risk not worth taking, my confidence in playing football at professional level was shot to pieces having been rejected so many times, what was going to change, whilst at 17 years and 9 months old I was still fit, I now had a potential career in Banking, which is exactly what it turned out to be.

However, I was firmly closing the final door on a potential football career by saying no, this haunted me for years and years to follow, I would never know if I could have made it to. I fell out of love with football.

When Kevin and Arthur invited me to a pre-season friendly against Doncaster Rovers at the old Belle View (no longer there) with Manchester City that I finally laid the ghost. I went into my old haunts the dressing room, the offices etc.

Kevin then took me down the tunnel towards the pitch and said this will be familiar. I suddenly stopped dead in my tracks, Kevin asked, "Are you ok?" I was filling up and getting quite emotional, I told him the last time I had been down that tunnel was in 1970 the day I was released.

He put his arm around me as we walked to the edge of the pitch and met up with Dave Penney the Doncaster Manager, he could see I was tearful, and Kevin explained.

That day laid the ghost of what might have been as a player and focused me for what lay ahead in my Scouting career, I had carried the burden around for many years, but I was now free at long last.

My branch manager called me into his office one day and said, "I understand you are a very good footballer, why are you not playing for the Bank." I explained and he said "Don't be stupid! The social side of banking can open doors for you and if you are as good as I have been told, it will help you get to know people."

So, I took his advice and joined the Banks football scene, what surprised me was the facilities they were far superior to Those at Belle View (Doncaster Rovers). There was under floor heating if I recall correctly at Norbury, and the pitches were first class.

The thing that I do remember from my first game was how many teams the Bank put out on a Saturday. It could be as many as 14/15 teams starting with the first team then at different levels all the way down to the bottom level.

I made my debut in the 6th team but, I'm not sure. I do remember I scored a couple of goals, and the captain came up to me as we walked off at full time and said, "Well you won't be playing for us next week", I asked why and he replied "You're far too good for us, we won't see you again." I think I had been started as high as the 6th level on pure hearsay and I had done well, so my career with the Banks football team was underway. I don't recall ever playing at level 6 or lower again, but I stand to be corrected on that fact.

But my career in professional football was well and truly over as a player.

However, in 1998 I did get involved in Professional Football when Kevin Keegan asked me to be part of his East Midlands scouting team at Fulham. I stayed with Fulham when Kevin left to join England and was part of the scouting team under Jean Tigana, we won promotion to the Premiership. That close season Kevin Keegan joined Manchester City in 2001 having left England and he asked me to join him again as they had been relegated from the Premiership ironically passing Fulham who went up.

I moved to Manchester City, and retired from there having enjoyed 19 years with the club in the scouting and recruitment department working for the first team.

I have worked for some really good managers during my time at Manchester City.

In particular, the last 10 years have been an amazing time and the success to be part of the team that has won 4 Premiership titles, not to mention F.A. Cups, League Cups and Community Shields.

City are now playing the best football I have ever seen and to be part of Pep's background staff was incredible, he is a perfectionist with his attention to detail.

When I finish with Manchester City, I think that will be that, nothing can compare with what I have been apart of, especially under Pep.

I feel I have been very lucky to have had two careers that I have enjoyed reaching the heights of Regional Manager in the regulated sales department in NatWest and finally, being involved at such a level in professional football.

3

NATWEST BANK AFC

The Playing Days

My reason for the prediction I made earlier, was my lifestyle. When I lived in London working for NatWest and playing football. After every game many of us, including, Dave Collard, Alan Webb, Howie Bristow, Paul Williams and Jim McLay, I will stop there so as not to upset anyone. We used to prop up the bar until our retrospective other halves would come and pick us up or we would catch the last train home - well oiled!

I was also playing football on a Sunday, for a good team run by Graham Shears, a good friend of mine whom I had met on an early training course, the team was called Thameside. I would repeat the process on a Sunday, then go back to work on Monday.

I worked in Sloane Square next to the King's Road and it was too easy to go for a drink after work instead of going straight home, especially on a Wednesday which was training night with NatWest. If you were in the first team or reserves, you were expected to turn up for training at Norbury catching a train from Victoria.

At the time my hair was long and jet black nearly down to my shoulders. I would often on a Wednesday have very good intentions to go training and my bag was duly packed.

I was living with a friend, Ian Collard, who had a house in Delboy country - Lanvannar Road, Peckham. Ian also played football for the bank like his brother Dave with whom I became great friends. We have visited them in Pairhares in France, about an hour and a half south of Lyon, where they moved some years ago.

We used to go to Dave and Margaret's for parties in Warlingham, Surrey where the Bacardi flowed. I remember the first time I visited them I sat down. Dave asked what I would like to drink, by now I had been introduced to Bacardi at Norbury, so that's what I asked for. Dave returned with a litre bottle of Coke, a large glass and a litre bottle of Bacardi. I started to pour two fingers, as it became known, of Bacardi which in truth measured about a third of the glass if not more topped up with ice and finally Coke. I went to give Dave back the bottles and he told me they were all mine.

Their parties were legendary and over the years we spent some great weekends with them, even going to the South of France in my little 1.2 Ford Fiesta driving down to St Tropez from Lincoln, trying to follow and keep up with them in his big bank 2.5 litre Rover. The Bacardi flowed again. So, you can see, I was burning the candle at both ends, that is why I made the prediction about not seeing 50.

As the years went by my lack of a desire to train, my long hair and my social life led to me being referred to as the 'George Best of NatWest'. I would often get to Victoria station look up at the train about to leave for Norbury, look at the pub, look back up at the train now due to leave in 2 minutes and head for the pub.

There came a time when my performances were dropping. Ian Roles and Roger Addems the team managers dropped a hint that I had better turn up for training now and again or I would not play. I took their advice.

But just finally on my time playing for the bank, I represented London against Wales (the date escapes me but was the early 70's) I scored a goal with a diving header I think we won 5-1. I never finished the game, in the course of scoring, as I dived to meet the cross being delivered from the left (where I should have been) the centre back came behind me and tried to clear the danger. I made contact with the ball first between the penalty spot and the six-yard box, his right boot connected with my head, as I rolled towards the post holding my face.

"Did I score?" I asked.

"Yes, you did - but bloody hell, you're covered in blood." came the reply.

I don't remember much more about that day (I'm sure there will be some out there that do) but I had received a detached retina in my right eye as a result of the kick to the head. Forty years ago, the treatment at St George's, Tooting was not what it is today but was at that time pioneering laser eye surgery. The surgeon obviously did a great job, as every time I go for my regular annual eye test, the comment is made how well the laser treatment has remained intact. I do have a slight gap in the corner of my eye which is the only real scar and is not obvious unless I point it out. That injury effectively finished me as a player.

I was out of action for 12 months, but told I should never play football again as an impact on my eye could result in blindness in that eye. Just over 12 months after the injury I made my comeback, I think for the reserves, and believe it or not I had kept reasonably fit.

I was of course a bit wary to start, especially about heading the ball. The game progressed I was feeling more confident, when I had to dive and head the ball again in the penalty box. The defender covering made contact again with my head, but all seemed well or so I thought, I did in fact suffer a slight reaction and blurred vision which put me back on the side-lines for a further 6 months. I do recall as I left the field at the end of that game someone coming up to me, who had seen the first incident some 12 months earlier and he said, "I was there 12 months ago and you have been kicked in the head again today, you are either extremely brave or f****** stupid!" He went on to add, "I think it's the latter." Some friends we have now would agree and I think they would add those kicks in my head explain lots of things about me. You all know who you are!

When I came back, I got injured again not long afterwards, with a cartilage problem I had torn my left cartilage in my knee, around December. I was told by the doctor that I would not play again that season which still had about five months left. Not sure how, but I was referred to the bank's specialist physiotherapist, I think this was because I got the injury playing for the bank!

On my first visit, she told me to do as I tell you and you will be playing again in 6 weeks. So, I for a change did as I was told and visited her, in bank time, every Tuesday at Russell Square, to go through my exercises. During the week I had to get a pair of oven gloves and put one weight into each pocket, a weight used in the bank for weighing silver, sit on the desk at work or on a chair at home and swing my leg up and down. I did this and other exercises religiously and to my surprise I was ready to play six weeks to the day. The only problem was I had put weight on this time around, as I was limited in my ability to exercise (nothing to do with the lager and Bacardi I had consumed during that period).

Ian 'Pod' Roles told me I was not playing until I lost the weight, so I was on a strict exercise programme (cut out the alcohol) and I was back in shape within a month or so (sure the lack of alcohol had no effect) it was just the exercise, I don't think!

I was ready again but the injuries one after another had made me very wary and whilst I never had another problem, I was never the same player at NatWest. I left to go back to Doncaster in 1978, I had fallen out of love with playing football again.

I played on and off after that for Doncaster area local clubs and eventually for Branston FC (the village I was living in near Lincoln since April 1984.). I continued playing as player/ manager and then manager of the first team. We won the Kelly Read trophy with a friend of mine, Richard Kwiatkowski, as joint manager he was an ex-pro who had played for Peterborough before joining NatWest bank, making the occasional appearance when we were short, but by now the weight was going on and not coming off. I continued until my son Paul who was born in 1982 started playing around 1992, at the age of 10. I of course went to watch him rather than be involved locally, until 1998 when I joined Fulham.

When I look back, I do believe before I joined Fulham, all these experiences had stood me in good stead for my career in professional scouting. I did not realise at the time, but I was building up a knowledge of football in many aspects. Little did I know what was in store though.

Hot Legs

Back in 1974, there were matches arranged against teams of Celebs called the 'ShowBiz XI'. We were asked as a Bank, if we would play against them at Norbury one Sunday, to give them some match practice before they embarked on a schedule of games raising money for charity.

I was invited to play in the game, and as the day arrived expectations were high, and everyone was looking forward to meeting some stars.

The day arrived and we were initially disappointed. When they started to arrive one by one, we recognised no one, they were a mixture of roadies and technical staff.

Eventually, Bill Oddie who gained fame with the Goodies and Junior Campbell, was the lead singer in the group The Marmalade, famous for the song, "Obla de Obla da," arrived, we were disappointed.

We were advised that kick-off was to be delayed, as they were waiting for their star player to arrive. We waited and eventually a stretch limo pulled into the car park.

Rod Stewart got out, that lifted our spirits. I was a fan of his music. In fact years later, I recorded an album just for fun and included the song "Maggie May."

We lined up for the kick-off, I was aware that Rod was a useful player who could have been a professional, in fact he was on Crystal Palace's books for a while.

I don't remember much about the game, but I do recall that after about ten minutes, Rod Stewart went past me dropping his shoulder as if I was not there. He had the look of a cross between George Best and Denis Law in his movement.

I wasn't having that, as he went past me, I was fairly quick and as he ran with the ball, I took his legs from behind. He went crashing to the ground turned and looked straight up at me, not very impressed.

A few minutes later he got his revenge as I went past him, he did the exact same to me, I could not complain, I deserved the same treatment. We smiled at each other and called it a draw and got on with the game. He truly was a very good player and showed that time and time again. I think we won 5-3 and I scored two goals but could not be sure on that.

At the final whistle we all shook hands and returned to the changing rooms.

What happened next, I used for my entire career in the bank and out of the bank when people used the "Tell us an interesting fact about yourself", line. I always said, "I once shared a bath with Rod Stewart!" I would then explain that after the match we all jumped into a large plunge bath that held around 20 people which was the norm in those days at pro-clubs, and with Norbury having better facilities than some pro-clubs, including Doncaster Rovers, this was a normal event after games.

Me and Rod sat in the bath and talked football, he told me he was going to Germany for the World Cup to watch Scotland play, this went on for about half an hour before we all got out and retired to the bar. I remember him saying how great it was that no one wanted to talk about his music, only his football, he loved the day.

I don't remember much about the rest of the day that was probably down to the amount of lager and Bacardi consumed during the rest of the day/evening.

I have told that story about the time spent with Rod in the bath on a regular basis and it always gets a good response, with the ladies thinking one thing and guys thinking something else if you know what I mean. My delivery of the story is what gives it that reaction, but all becomes clear in the end and everyone smiles as reality of the situation becomes clear.

Gambling whilst Working for the Bank

Whilst I worked in the banking industry you would think we bank employees would have more sense than gamble, but you would be wrong, there were also a few who took it further and got into ownership syndicates.

From memory, a really nice guy called Bob Coomes had a share in a racehorse called Nonon. I don't think we were supposed to be involved at such a level, and again from memory Bob was a bank inspector, which made things worse as he should have known better but, everyone turned a blind eye, everyone feared the inspectors walking into your branch to do a full check on procedures.

They were the only people in the bank allowed to use certain colour pens to indicate and report on their findings. Anyway, I always backed Bob's horse every time it ran, and I think it was only ever placed once, I may be wrong on that statistic, but I had it each way at 100/1.

As I say, it was a long time ago around the early to mid-70s, but I recall watching it run often before we went out to play. It was a sprinter, the fastest horse I have ever seen over three to four furlongs it was often well clear of its field.

Unfortunately, horse races in the UK are run over a minimum of 5 furlongs, and by the time Nonon had got to the winning post it was either last or nearly last, it would just basically run out of legs as it entered the final furlong, Bob and the others involved got rid of it eventually to China I believe.

Around the same time for some unknown reason three people who all played football for the bank decided to buy a greyhound. Ted Taylor, Roger Addems and yes, yours truly. As far as money was concerned, I was the younger less well paid getting married person of the three, and could ill afford to spend money on such a thing, but I did.

I can't remember how much we paid for the first Dog we purchased, but I paid my third of the costs. It was a young black dog with a kennel name of Della. The training was going well, and she showed some real ability and was progressing well. We even had names suggested based on the breeding, you normally try and combine the names of the parents. Names such as the current NatWest Bank chairman was offered, but quickly dismissed as not to ruffle any senior bank official feathers

One other name mentioned based on its parentage was to call it Passing Wind. Again, dismissed. I thought it was quite good. In the end, it turned out we never got to actually register a name, which I will explain.

Nearing her time to race, you have to get the dog qualified by running over the same distance at least three times to get a basis for what level it can enter into graded races, the better the times the higher up the grading system it goes They usually run from a low of around grade 6 or 7 up to grade one then if it really is a star it gets to run in what is called open races where the serious prize money can be won.

Della was ready for her final trial at Crayford and Roger Addems was going to watch and report back. I was waiting with excited nervousness, you name it I was suffering with it, waiting for the news.

The word filtered through as follows. She fell out of the traps stumbled and by the first corner was a good 15 to 20 lengths behind the other two dogs in a three-dog trial. Down the back straight, she turned on the pace and by the time the three dogs were coming to the final bend she had passed one of the dogs and was closing fast on the remaining dog, apparently the people watching were amazed and gasped in appreciation at how this dog had recovered from such a terrible start to be now about to take the lead and win quite easily. Looks like we have a serious dog on our hands.

However, as Della came to pass the remaining dog to take the lead, she broke one of greyhound racings commandments as she drew level with the leader. She turned her head towards the other dog and attacked it by trying to bite it (even though they wear muzzles this is a no no).

The crowd watching were now gasping for a different reason, this meant that Della was now sine die from racing (effectively barred and given a life ban). Having shown this trait once, she could never be trusted. The dream that had shown promise down the back straight was now in tatters.

Was that the adventure over?

No.

What happened next gave us great fun.

Blessington Sky. Breeding Skyhawk out of Lady Blessington. The Perfect Name.

We got together to decide what to do next. A trainer called Ingram-Seal trained dogs at Maidstone and had been mentioned to one of us I think it may have been Roger. We all went with our partners to Maidstone one Friday night to take things further.

He started to tell us he had two dogs for sale both were running that evening in kennel semi-finals one was Blessington Sky a lovely big brindle dog with a very long nose, he was running in the second semi.

The other dogs name which I do not recall, was running in the first semi.

The first semi was run, and the dog finished 4th which meant it had not made the final.

Next up was Blessington he ran well and finished 3rd so made the final. Both dogs were low to medium graders, so we were not going to make a fortune, it was just a bit of fun.

Myself and Lynda with Blessington

The trainer said the first dog is up for sale at £400.

Blessington, who made the final had been left in the kennels by its owner and the trainer just wanted to clear the outstanding kennel bill. As the owner had just left the dog with him and he had all the paperwork to switch the dog to new owners. We asked how much the bill was and he said £90.

After a short group chat we agreed to buy the dog and looked forward to seeing him run in the final the following Friday.

Honestly, the dog itself seemed to perk up as we all made a fuss of it, stroking it talking to it as you do.

So, we waited all week waiting for the day and headed for Maidstone greyhound track.

The time came and Blessington's race was next. He opened as one of the outsiders at around 9/2. As usual, I had to have a bet £10 was a lot of money then for me, but I had it on at 9/2. He flew out of the traps and was in front at the first bend, passed the winning post but with one more circuit still to go, down the back straight he was still in front as he came to the last bend, he took it great keeping tight, we were going daft shouting and screaming for all we were worth. The next part is a blur but believe it or not he hung on to win.

We were all going crazy, we had only won a few quid. In fact I won more than the prize money, my bet had returned a profit of £45 which more than covered my cost to buy the dog. We also got a small trophy.

You would have thought we had won the greyhound derby. The trainer came to us with a surprised look on his face and I remember vividly him saying, "That dog has not won a race for over two years, I just can't believe it! You have it for a week and it wins, it has been much happier since last Friday when you all made a fuss of it".

Perhaps that is what FLASH (his kennel name) needed someone to have confidence in him, you just don't know.

From there he did ok and we learnt a lot about his character. For example, he preferred to be in trap 1 or 2 as he was what is called a railer as opposed to a middle track runner in traps 3 or 4 with greyhounds in traps 5 or 6 designated as wide runners.

If he missed the break and found himself at the first bend in say 4th or 5th he would just drop out as he did not like sand kicked in his face, on the other hand if he was in the front two at the first bend then he would try and stay there.

One race at Maidstone stands out and I was not there to see it. Again, a Friday night we had been advised by the trainer Mr Ingram-Seal that he had a great chance of winning now that he had found some form and was expected to start as a 6/4 Favourite. I had my customary bet but this time I had put £20 to win so expected a return of £30 profit.

I even rang my father who lived in a small mining village called Edlington near Doncaster, South Yorkshire who loved a pint and a bet to put some money on Blessington.

He promptly told all his mining friends in the village who like a bet and many of them put some money on with William Hill in the local village betting shop. No such thing as online internet betting. Anyway, the money was on, so I was just waiting for the result.

Roger Addems, I think who was at the track, rang with the result. He had WON but not at 6/4 but at 10/1!

They had replaced some of the runners with reserves and he was not the good thing as expected so his price drifted. However, as we were all on at starting price, we would get 10/1 so I was collecting £200.

My father was the toast of the local working men's club as many of them had also backed the dog. However, when they went to pick up their winnings on the Saturday Morning William Hill were holding all bets whilst they investigated the result.

Think about it a small mining village in South Yorkshire taking around 10 or so bets on a dog race in Maidstone Kent, all on one dog with an SP of 10/1 well suspicious or what.

It turned out there had been a gamble that night on various dogs which were being investigated but it did not involve Blessington.

So, everyone got paid out to say Blessington gave the Yorkshire miners a good weekend is an understatement.

For reasons I won't go into, we switched Blessington to a track in Catford and he had to trial again to get in. This time the distance was up from 460 yards to 525 yards, he had never run over that distance but managed to scrape in and qualify to race. I remember his first race well.

He had been used to an outside hare, but this time it was an inside hare and he was in trap 6 so everything was against him as he liked to run near the inside rails.

The first bend was not very far from the start, and the dogs had to go around the track, past the starting position and round the last bend towards the finishing line.

The traps went up and Blessington flew from the traps and was in front after two or three strides, he reverted to type and headed across the others towards the hare which was on the inside in line with trap one. Well to say it was carnage you had to see it to believe it, he left behind him dogs crashing into each other which meant he was in the lead as they passed the finishing line for the first time with a complete circuit to go by some 20 lengths, what he had done was not illegal just part of greyhound racing.

The others were now chasing him, as he got to the start position, he was still 10 to 15 lengths clear, but the rest were closing fast, he was getting into untried territory for the last 50 yards or so.

As they came around the bend towards the finish line trap four, the favourite, was drawing level with him. He dug in and pulled out more, they crossed the line together. Remember earlier I mentioned he had a very long nose, well it paid off he won by the shortest distance you could imagine after a long wait for the result of the photofinish.

I had my customary £10 on him but for some reason I also did the forecast. His starting price was 10/1, so with £100 profit plus the forecast, I had another profitable night thanks to Blessington. Plus of course the prize money which was better than Maidstone.

We went to see him and bless him as he saw us he wagged his tail, bleeding from one paw and was gasping for air he was knackered I swear he looked up at all of us and was thinking what the f*** was that all about?

Blessington had never run that far in his life before; he was panting very hard. He rarely lost when he got in front, but the distance was too far for him, and I think we all knew that. He never won another race at Catford and when I left London with the bank to return to Doncaster, he eventually came with me.

He won a couple of races at Doncaster track before getting badly injured and I had to have him put down. I was devastated and shattered. He had given me so much pleasure not to mention the money he never cost me a penny and he only cost me £30 to buy a share.

When he ever had a chance of winning, he tried his heart out if he had no chance after the first few yards, he would just drop out the back, so he didn't get sand in his face. He was not stupid, why bother. He seemed to say, I will wait till next time.

Thanks, Blessington Sky.

The Wedding

I feel I ought to mention my wedding on the 6th September 1975, when a NatWest Bank team made up of many of my mates from London, attended my wedding in Doncaster. They partied on Saturday before playing football on the Sunday against a NWB team from Doncaster.

Needless to say, I don't remember much about the day.

However, I do remember when I was in the church on the Saturday, waiting for Lynda. The guys from London entered the church and I remember hearing Paul Williams say

"It's nice in here," I turned and saw him walking down the aisle to his seat smoking a big cigar. I thought bl**** hell, what's he doing smoking in a catholic church? At that point Jim McLay came in and I heard Jim say, "Any friend of batman is a friend of mine", he was referring to my cousin, Sister Ignatius, who was a nun from Melton Mowbray and in her full habit playing the organ. I was now getting nervous as to what would happen next!

To make matters worse I also heard Jim McLay say as the altar boys rang the bells, "Jesus is that last orders already?"

As it happened, I apparently married myself. When I said to the priest, "I John Starrs take thee John Starrs (instead of Lynda Mitchell) to be my lawful wedded wife." So, to this day I'm not sure if I am married or not.

We all had a good night with plenty of free booze which went down well.

The next morning, with a game to play, I have to say the London boys did not look at their best. Lynda and I both went to watch the game before heading off to Scotland on honeymoon.

I went into the dressing room prior to kick off to find more than one of the London boys with their head in their hands, especially Bert Leen, who when handed the number ten shirt said "I can't wear that."

"Why not?" he was asked.

"Two numbers are far too heavy in my state" came the reply.

By half time more than one of my teammates were struggling, so I was told you better get changed you're on in the second half, I had been married less than 24 hours, and now I was going to play football.

I went on and I was put through on goal, one v one with the keeper, I duly slotted the ball through his legs into the net.

One shout from the side lines was heard,

"STARRZY!......bet that's the first time you have scored twice in two days" - everyone fell about laughing.

I don't remember the final score, but I think we won the game against Doncaster to everyone's surprise.

When I returned to work in Bawtry near Doncaster in 1978, I was persuaded to play for Doncaster area in the local area competitions, we had mixed success, but I quite enjoyed the occasional game.

After the game, Lynda and I went north to Scotland and the guys went south to London. The event was discussed for a long time afterwards at Norbury, usually starting with the phrase "Do you remember".

The Double Nutmeg

I must tell the story about the double nutmeg, we were playing a game and I was playing wide on the left, an opportunity came near the halfway line to slot the ball through an opponent's legs, behind him, in direct line was Jim McLay. Jim was a talented player and a great character, who was on Falkirk's books at one time.

As I slotted the ball through the opponent's legs I shouted 'NUTMEG', the player had spun round and was now facing Jim, he was about 4 or 5 feet away. Jim shouted so everyone could hear "AND AGAIN" with a first-time ball, straight back through his legs. Needless to say, the other player was not amused. I fell about laughing as the ball reached me, only to be clattered and ended up on my back over the touchline. I was still laughing when the referee added insult to injury and booked the opposition player for the tackle.

I had never seen a double nutmeg before or since even at the highest level, but Jim was quick thinking and I will never ever forget it. Thanks for the memory that I was part of Jim.

The week after we played the same team again and my uncle was down from Scotland and both he and Lynda came to watch. As we arrived, I caught a glimpse of the player involved from the previous week, when he saw me, he did not look happy. As we were going into the changing room, he came up to me.

"Don't even think of trying that again or I will clatter you," he said.

I went to get changed and on leaving the changing rooms I said to Lynda and my uncle that the guy in the double nutmeg story was playing and he had warned me. I said "keep an eye out I have something up my sleeve, but I will signal you before I do it." They looked at me quizzically and somewhat confused.

Just before we lined up for the kick-off he was on my side of the field, in a wide midfield position and I was a wide left sided attacker, so again, we were in direct line with each other.

I told him just after kick-off, when the ball was out of play that I was going to nutmeg him again, but this time it would be just me involved, that my girlfriend and uncle were on the touchline watching the game, and I was going to signal to them when I was going to nutmeg him. He was not amused! The game progressed and we had a few skirmishes but nothing serious, I had to wait my time, as I knew I would only get one chance. I have to say it was affecting my game, but then during the first half my chance came. I got the ball around the half way line wide on the left, he came towards me and this was my chance, with him about 4 or 5 feet away, I stopped, put my foot on the ball and raised an arm and shouted to Lynda and my uncle, "NOW THE NUTMEG!".

The player looked like the metaphorical 'rabbit caught in headlights' as I said to him now is the time. I quickly shouted "NUTMEG" and put the ball through his legs and ran around him. I could hear him swearing as I went past him, and as I got on the ball, I knew what was coming next. He took me out from behind with a vicious challenge, but all I did was laugh as I hit the ground. I deserved the tackle in truth, I had made him look stupid for the second time in a week.

After the game I went towards him to shake his hand and apologise, he took it in good spirit, and we shared a drink in the bar later. He did say he could not believe he had been caught out again, that was why he had made the rash tackle, I said to him

"I don't blame you with my record I probably would have been sent off twice, thought you took it really well."

England v Scotland

Lynda reminded me of a story from when I was working in London. I went to Wembley (which I did quite often) and sometimes I would get tickets from Kevin to watch England against Scotland. He said to me once that I'd got the cheek of the devil getting him to supply me with match tickets for England games when he knew I was born in Glasgow and was going to support Scotland! We laughed about it but, there can't be many people who get tickets from an England player then went and supported the opposition.

The match on the 4th June 1977 will be remembered for the day that Scotland fans wrecked Wembley after beating England 2-1. Kevin had arranged for me to pick up a ticket from Emlyn Hughes. Along with members of my family, it became a tradition that we stayed with Dave Collard. We would all go to the game and have a party afterwards. We also went to Scotland from time to time and did the same.

On that day, in June 1977, Wembley was overrun with Scotland supporters. I took up my seat near the halfway line and a few minutes later, a Scotsman who I had never met before joined me. Everybody was searched on the way to their seat. He quickly put his hand inside his jacket and pulled out a half bottle of scotch, which we started to share.

I asked how he got it past the security guards, he told me that as he was about to be searched, he shouted, "There's a fight over there" and walked off as they turned away to look and they never stopped him.

By kick off, the stadium was full to bursting with over 98,000 fans and most of them were Scottish. At half time we had nearly finished the half bottle of whisky, so I took him to the bar and bought a few more drinks.

I don't really remember the second half! All I know is that Scotland won 2-1, the fans went wild and invaded the pitch wrecking the goal posts and digging up the pitch, which ended up in the gardens of some fans, to remember the day.

Whilst I do not condone this sort of behaviour, it was not aggressive towards the England fans who were there, not many I must add, but celebrating a win against the auld enemy.

I thought best to get away and meet up with my friend Dave Collard and family. As we left my fellow Scot, who I had spent the day with and was now singing as happy as Larry, suddenly said, "Watch this." His face changed and he started to look as if he was crying. I thought what's the matter with him? He was happy and smiling a few seconds ago.

He came up in front of a policeman and said to him, in a tearful manner, "Officer I have lost my brother and he has got the tickets home,"

"Oh right, what does he look like? The officer asked.

"He has a tartan scarf and a tartan tammy (hat)", my friend said with a dead straight face.

The policeman saw the funny side and realised he had been caught, he said to my friend well done now move on and smiling as he said it. We said our farewells and went our separate ways.

I met up with my family and friends and headed for the Underground, to say it was chaos does not do it justice. However, as we got near to the train that was pulling into the station the doors opened the fans parted and let this one lone guy through, past the entire queue. We held the door for him and could see he was holding his arm which was in a sling and he had a very pained expression on his face.

Supporters were shouting let this man through he is in pain and has a broken arm. The man thanked them and got on the tube. Somebody offered him his seat, he politely refused but continued to look in pain.

As the train doors closed and pulled away, he slipped his arm out of the sling to reveal a bottle of scotch, which he offered around saying

"I was at the back of the queue and would have been ages to get on the tube I was not going to stand around and wait for ever."

There was nothing wrong with him. Everybody smiled and laughed as they sang, "They scored one. We scored two. Big Don Revie's on the brew!" (the dole in Scotland) again and again and again.

We had a great night back at Dave and Margaret Collard's. He was adopted as an honorary Scot and my family enjoyed many a good time in both Scotland and at Dave and Margaret's in years to follow.

Kevin Keegan, a Carnation & who will win the FA Cup?

On the 1st May 1976 Southampton met Manchester United in the FA Cup Final.

But I want to take you back to the days just before the Cup final starting with Thursday the 29th April.

I had arranged to go to the Hyde Park Hotel to meet up with Kevin and his wife Jean before he went off to receive his award for the Sports Writers Player of the Year.

When I arrived at the hotel Kevin had a carnation in his hand that he was trying to put into his lapel before leaving for the award ceremony. Jean was not going so they said why don't you stay and have a meal with Jean and a representative from Shoot Magazine, I readily agreed.

Lynda was at home in Bromley having beans on toast, she was not amused!

Kevin disappeared for a few minutes coming back with no carnation on his jacket, he remarked I paid £££'s for that and it fell apart, and I could have got a bunch of carnations in Doncaster for what I paid for that one. We all laughed.

We sat down and had a general chat and the subject of the F.A.Cup Final came up. At this point Kevin revealed that he was going to be on the panel of experts who would discuss the game on a programme which went out on the eve of the Cup Final, it was very popular in the 70's hosted by Brian Moore called " Who will win the Cup."

Kevin thought for some reason that Southampton would win despite being underdogs and went on to give his reasons why. Think he had been talking to his great friend Mick Channon who said they were up for the game, with nothing to lose.

He left for the award ceremony without a carnation in his lapel...

I stayed, had dinner and they would not let me pay so, Shoot magazine picked up the bill.

I made my farewells and headed for the train home.

The next morning on my way to work I called early to the Hyde Park Hotel in Knightsbridge as I worked very near in Sloane Square. I had a bunch of flowers (Carnations) for Jean as a way of a thank you for the dinner the previous evening.

I also had one carnation separate with Baco foil around the stem for Kevin with a message you can wear this one tonight in your lapel on Television with Brian Moore and Co.

The format of the show was that Brian Moore would have four guests round a table discussing the Cup Final and they would all discuss the game. Initially, they would be asked who they thought would win the Cup.

I sat down with Lynda to watch the programme, incidentally on the strength of my conversation with Kevin I had a bet on Southampton at good odds being the underdogs to win the cup in 90 minutes.

The first thing I noticed as the panel were being introduced was that Kevin had my Carnation in his lapel. I gave a little smile to, myself.

The program started and Kevin was the last of the four other guests to give his opinion. The first guest said surprisingly Southampton would win as did the next two guests.

This left Kevin as the final guest to give his opinion, I remember at this point turning to Lynda, well that's all of them going for

Southampton.

At this point Kevin said, "Southampton have no chance, United will win easily."

I was stunned, the night before he was so adamant that Southampton would win. I looked at Lynda, she looked at me in disbelief and I was confused. Anyway, Kevin gave his rational which was the total opposite to what we had discussed the previous evening.

The next day I sat down and watched Southampton with players such as Mick Channon, Peter Osgood and Bobby Stokes who scored the winner in the 83rd minute. Southampton were under the management of Laurie McMenemy, my last manager at Doncaster Rovers.

On the Monday I phoned Kevin at home in Molde and asked him "What made you change your mind?"

He replied, "I didn't change my mind."

When he got to the studio it transpired that all four guests thought Southampton would win. The producers said that's no good someone must go for United.

Kevin said the four guests had to draw lots for one of them to give United the vote and he was the one that lost out and had to make a case for Manchester United to win the cup.

I replied, "I will never watch or believe anything I see or hear on television again!"

The £3000 Watch

Before I had stopped working, I attended an Area Managers meeting, I was sat on a round table with other area managers near the end of the night having a beer or two.

Someone said, "Have you seen my new watch? It cost me £1500."

"Mine cost £1900", said another and so on these, were much younger than me and lacked experience in the real world, to them it was all about the material benefits.

By this time, having listened to this b******* I stood up and asked in a loud voice to all on the table pointing to my watch.

"Can I just check the time?"

They all replied, "It's 10.30."

"That's very funny mine also says 10.30 and it only cost £20," I quipped, at which point I turned and went to bed leaving them bemused.

Since the takeover by the RBS Group, I could see problems coming and these pretentious individuals were the future; which I was glad I was no longer a part of when I retired.

When RBS took over NatWest, I felt we lost focus on the basics, and it became all about targets. Another correct decision.

How lucky am I?

4

THE PHONE CALL THAT CHANGED MY LIFE

It all started as a hobby that grew and grew over the years. It also happened not because what I knew, but who I knew as they say.

I went to school with Kevin Keegan and we kept in touch after we left St Peter's Catholic School in Cantley near Doncaster. Through his days at Scunthorpe United to Liverpool, Hamburg, Southampton, Newcastle and England. We are still in touch and speak now and again just to catch up.

In January 1998, I was living in Lincoln and I received a phone call from Kevin. At the time, he was manager of Fulham; with his great friend, the late great Ray Wilkins. He asked me if I could go and watch a player who played for Lincoln at the time. I went along and watched this player with my son Paul, who always pestered me to take him to Lincoln. After the game, I told Kevin what I thought. His response to me was,

"Starrzy, (still calls me that) that's the same as the reports we have on him."

Kevin asked me to do another report the following week. So, the following Saturday I went and did a report on another player. I sent it to him the following day, and he rang me up later. He asked me if I wanted to do some work for him and Arthur Cox as they hadn't got a scout in the East Midlands.

He warned me in advance that if I didn't come up to scratch, I would be told. Scouting in a football club was and still is a very important part of any club as they are the men and women who look for the next generation of talent.

I agreed to take in games at the weekend, as I was in full time employment with NatWest in the Regulated Sales Department. It all started from there, as a hobby. To be honest, it was a welcome break from banking, and I only received expenses, no payment of any kind.

My first game was at Mansfield Town and I picked out a couple of players of interest. I heard nothing back from Kevin or Arthur. I was then asked to do a match analysis report on up and coming opposition. This was far more complicated than just watching one player. I had to report on formations used, both attacking and defensively and in transition. Give individual pen pictures of the starting eleven, giving a short summary as to which foot they used, pace, physical ability, strength and weaknesses, not only as individuals but as a team. Over time this developed and became a 20+ page document to be analysed prior to the game. The most difficult part was getting the set pieces down. For example, an attacking corner they need to know (and still do) the taker, where everybody is in and out of the box and the movement of all players. It's not as easy as you may think, try it next time you watch a game either on tv or better still, live.

After six or seven weeks I'd heard nothing, so I phoned Kevin to ask him what the situation was. He said, "Has Arthur not rung you?". When I told him that he hadn't, Kevin told me,

"Then you're doing great. If Arthur has not needed to contact you, then take that as a compliment".

In all honesty I learned on the job. I learnt how to obtain the information and get into a routine. My routine was I always tried (and generally succeeded) in arriving at games to be covered at least one hour before kick-off to watch the warmup. It is surprising what you can find out from observing the players, whether it was an individual player or a team report. The first thing to get is the formation of the team you're watching. To do this, you must be able to identify the players. I used to do this by looking for different colour boots, different hairstyles, how long their shirt sleeves were.

The following piece of advice I was given by Arthur Cox which has stood me in good stead was as follows:

Write what you see - not what you want to see.

Keep yourself to yourself.

The information you have is for us to know and others to find out.

Whilst this may sound strange, I soon understood what Arthur meant. Many scouts seemed to be on an ego trip, wanting to tell you who they had seen lately, what they had said about certain players, where they had been, who they had recommended.

They wanted people to know if their club signed the player, they'd played a part in the decision. It was surprising what people told me.

I have kept that advice to myself and stuck by it ever since.

My first season under Kevin, Ray Wilkins and Arthur Cox finished with Fulham who were in what is now League One. We finished 6th in the league, meaning we entered the play offs. We played 3rd placed Grimsby Town and lost over two legs; missing out on a chance for promotion to the Championship.

"I Can't Find You"

Speaking of Grimsby, Kevin once invited me along to an away game at Grimsby. You didn't often get to see your own team play. After the game as we were leaving, a couple of supporters approached Kevin to ask for a photo. As always, he obliged and got me to take the photo for them. I lined them up and was ready to take the snapshot until I looked through the camera and couldn't see the three waiting for me to click the camera.

I brought the camera down and said, "I can't find you". Kevin quick as a flash (no pun intended) replied,

"He is one of our scouts, if he can't find you from four feet, what chance does he have of finding a player?"

They all laughed again at my expense.

I think by now you will notice that a pattern is emerging, but I give as good as I get.

The Most Expensive Burger

Teams often stay in hotels the night before a match, but there are strict instructions about diet & drinking etc. On one occasion, a certain player was still hungry around 11.00 pm and decided to order a burger and chips. The burger arrived and he signed for it on his room number.

On the Monday, the manager got hold of the receipts and noticed the entry for the burger. He called the player concerned into his office and confronted the player, who did not deny it.

"Why didn't you pay cash?" the manager asked.

"I never thought!"

"If you'd paid cash I would never have known." (trying to give him a hint).

As we both know I must fine you now, or the others will think they can get away with similar things. The player accepted the reasoning and the fine, which was said to be around £500.

Season 1998/99 – League One

	1998/99 Table	GD	Points
1	Fulham	+47	101
2	Walsall	+16	87
3	Manchester City	+36	82

The following season, which was the clubs 101st season in professional football, under Kevin and Arthur, we totally dominated the League One title, winning the league by 14 points.

Ironically, it matched the 101st season in football for the club. You could say it was meant to be. Manchester City finished 3rd in the division, and we lost to Manchester United 1-0 in the 5th round of the F.A. Cup with again, ironically Andrew Cole scoring the goal, a player whom Kevin had sold to them when he was at Newcastle United.

On the last day of the season Lynda and I, along with other scouts, were invited down to Craven Cottage to celebrate our promotion. Every time I see The Cottage on TV, it brings back memories. Lynda always says, "been in that cottage!"

We had lunch prior to the game at a local Italian restaurant on the Fulham Road, and were rewarded with both Kevin and Arthur being present to say a big thank you to all involved. That is the measure of them even prior to a game, they made time for the people who had been involved.

After the game, we attended a celebration party at Harrods. It was hosted by the owner Mohamed al Fayed. No expense was spared, we were collected from our hotel and taken to a private door at the side of Harrods. It was all very surreal. The store was closed completely, we were led through the store and up an escalator to a large door which when opened, revealed a big room with large round tables. The tables were filled with food from every country you could imagine, served from what you could describe as cookie stalls and with a free bar, with the champagne flowing.

Mohamed Al Fayed made sure he welcomed everyone. Kevin introduced me to him, and all night he walked around talking to everyone making sure they were having a great time and if your glass was getting low, then someone came and filled it up all night. An evening never to be forgotten.

I was on my way - could it get any better than this?

1999-2001 – The Championship

However, it was an uncertain time as Kevin had given his word in February, that at the end of that season, he would take the England job and was therefore leaving Fulham. He kept his word and was replaced by Paul Bracewell, so I did not know whether I still had a job. I had no need to worry as Paul Bracewell was fully aware of my previous input and I was retained.

However, that did not last long. In April 2000, he was replaced by the former French international, Jean Tigana, who took over for the 2000/01 season.

Fulham's Victorious Championship Winning Season 2000/01

Won	30
Goal Difference	+58
Points	101

This was again a concern as to whether I still had a role to play, but again I was asked to continue doing player and match reports on the opposition. We had a record-breaking season winning the 2000/2001 Championship and getting promoted to the Premiership for the season starting 2001/2002.

I was pleased that having been recruited by Kevin, I was still there on merit it seemed.

As the 2001/02 season approached, everything and everyone were good to go for the new season in the Premiership with Fulham. This was the first time the club had been back in the topflight of English football since 1968, and it would be their home until 2014.

However, Kevin's reign as England manager did not turn out as he had hoped, he was a free agent and Manchester City had been relegated under Joe Royle in 2001.

Kevin and Arthur took over at Manchester City during the close season for the season 2001/02.

Jokingly, one Sunday morning I was sitting in my lounge with Lynda and my son, Paul. I was teasing them saying I would contact Kevin to see if he wanted me to join MCFC. They had gone down and passed Fulham, ironically, who had gone up.

They both replied in unison,

"You must be crazy, why go back down to the Championship when you have just been promoted to the Premiership?!"

I was of course only teasing; I had no intention of phoning Kevin.

A few days later, my son answered the phone (it was usually for him anyway). He said, "Kevin Keegan wants to speak to you Dad."

I assumed he was getting his own back at first. I would not take the phone. I thought he had got someone to ring me to wind me up. However, he got more and more agitated as I refused to take the phone. Eventually, I did and to my surprise, it was Kevin. He said, "I would like you to come and join us at Manchester City."

This was a request from Arthur Cox and not coming just from Kevin. He also said it did not come purely off the back of our friendship, as it is a big task at Manchester City, and they needed people, willing to work, even on a part time basis, to stabilize the club. He said think it over and get back to him. To say I was in shock is an understatement. In truth, while it was going to be a wrench to leave Fulham, it really did not take me long to return to Kevin and accept his offer. At that point, Kevin told me Arthur Cox had specifically asked him to contact me due to our friendship.

"This will be the biggest compliment you ever get in football, Arthur does not do this normally, so be honoured."

Suffice to say, I was bowled over and he was right. I was and am still honoured.

We agreed terms and left it with both Kevin and Arthur to sort things out with Fulham and the chief scout, John Marshall. I felt bad, especially when John rang me and said, "I won't make this easy, as we do not want you to leave, what can we do to keep you?"

I was flattered but, in view of my friendship with Kevin, I could not turn it down, which he understood and thought that would be the case. John and I remain good friends to this day and he is currently chief scout at Wolverhampton Wanderers.

My time at Fulham had come to an end. I was happy that I had been part of the scouting and recruitment department that had won two titles ending up in the Premiership between January 1998 and May 2001. Some scouts never have the fortune or luck to win one title, never mind two in such a short time.

How lucky I was.

Being part of a club like Fulham and Manchester City from time to time you get an invite to an evening with a retired footballer who does some after dinner speaking, this was the case whilst I was in my early days at Fulham.

Grimsby Town invited me along to one such event with Peter Osgood and Tommy Smith as guest speakers.

To our surprise, we were placed on the top table with Lynda and I in between the two great players.

Peter Osgood (top) & Tommy Smith (below)

Following a three-course meal they both did their routine which included some very strong language, but to be fair Tommy warned Lynda and others present there would be.

This was followed by an auction of memorabilia to raise funds for charity.

Unfortunately both are no longer with us, Peter passed away on the 1st March 2006 at the age of 59. Tommy passed away recently on the 12th April 2019 at the age of 74.

God bless you both.

5

TWO STEPS FORWARD, ONE STEP BACK

In the short time I had at Fulham, I'd been part of the team involved in a semi-final play-off against Grimsby Town, winners of the League One title and winners of the Championship. Not a bad start to my scouting career.

Now I was about to take a step back into the Championship with Manchester City and try to help get them back into the Premiership.

I had learnt a lot from my first experience at Fulham which was going to be crucial in the coming years. Manchester City were going places and as it turned out, I was there right at the start of the journey.

They had been a club living in the shadows of United (can't bear to say M********* United). But first we had to get back into the Premiership under Kevin, Arthur Cox and coach Derek Fazakerley (or Faz as he was better known). We also had Stuart Pearce as club captain. On paper a great team, and I was part of that team, along with other scouts, some of whom had been scouting for the club for more than 30 years. One of whom was Willie O'Donnell, who sadly died a few years ago but not before he had enjoyed the last remaining of his years with a successful team. This had not been the case for most of his time at City, always struggling to maintain topflight status, never mind win anything.

Another long serving scout at the club was a Scottish former professional, John Ferguson. He is still with the club and still going to games aged 79 (he has forgotten more than I will ever know). They were more involved with the youth side, bringing players into the club, who over the years became household names.

A picture of John Ferguson, left, & John Graveling, right

Some of the other scouts included: Rod Cousins, who was a retired teacher; Alex Owen, who had his own stage sound business, working in places like Las Vegas with Elton John and Celine Dion among others. Alex, I believe was a millionaire in his own right, but you would never know a more gentle and humble man you could ever wish to meet. In addition, there was Ralph Wright, a former professional; Peter Morris, a former player and manager at the POSH, along with a few other clubs.

We were a tight team with Rod and me mainly used for opposition match analysis reporting. Between us, we always did three reports on the up and coming opposition.

A few years later, another retired teacher John Graveling joined us from Sheffield United and quickly settled in. He took a share of the match reports, as well as looking for players like Rod and myself.

Steve Burtenshaw was another one of the team. He was a very experienced scout and had joined Manchester City after me. He was an ex-Brighton player and had been manager at Sheffield Wednesday, Everton, QPR and Arsenal.

He had been brought in by Arthur as well, but was from the very old school of scouting, he only did players, no match reports and did not get on well with technology, which in the end played its part in him retiring earlier than he should.

Steve was from the school that wrote things down on the back of a fag packet or just phoned up and someone else, I think, would put his report onto the Scout 7 system. He was another example of someone who had forgotten more than I will ever know about football, I learnt a lot from just listening to him. Steve had some great stories. I remember him relating a story about Stan Bowles when he was at QPR; and what a character Stan was.

Stan had been called up to the England squad and the night before in the hotel they would have meetings with potential sponsors. Steve was also at the hotel and recalls seeing Stan in discussion with a very high-profile boot company. Later, he was seen with another high-profile boot company shaking hands with both as they left the hotel some 45 minutes apart. The next day all was to become clear Stan had agreed a deal with both companies and ran out at Wembley wearing two different boots, he had secured sponsorship from both, typical Stan. Stan would often be seen in his kit in the local bookmakers prior to and after the game.

Steve recalled on one occasion, on the day of the Grand National, he kept the ball in the corner as the race was developing. He got a supporter who was listening to the race on his radio to keep him informed of how his horse was getting on (not sure I believe that story, but Steve did tell it convincingly).

Steve told me that when he was a player, one summer in the close season, he picked up his wages to find he'd only been paid half the amount he was expecting. He went to see his manager to ask why. The reply he got was, "In the close season you are only half as good as you are in the normal season, so that's why you only get paid half as much."

What could Steve say, he just turned and walked out of the manager's office. Can you imagine that happening today?

Steve effectively retired early not because of lack of competence, but because he could not keep up with the onset of the fast-growing reliance on technology required to compile reports.

He is, I believe 82, and he retired to the South coast.

This was something I took on board, if someone with his knowledge could be retired on those grounds, I had better keep up with all developments in technology if I wanted to stay in the game. I was proved right; changes were coming thick and fast as I was to experience and thankfully embrace.

These were the main scouts; the others were casual people working with the youth and academy teams. I worked for the first team from my start at Fulham, not really looking at players below the age of 17.

That suited me having been released by Doncaster Rovers in 1970 and rejected earlier by managers such as Joe Harvey (Newcastle United), Ian Greaves (Huddersfield Town), Tommy Docherty (Rotherham United) and Lawrie McMenemy (Doncaster Rovers). I always said that at least I was rejected by some of the best managers at the time.

Incidentally, I was taken on at Doncaster Rovers, as a 15-year-old, by

George Raynor. When I tell people his name, I usually get a blank look, but he was probably the most experienced manager of them all in many ways. I can hear people saying, "Who is he?"

Well, he was manager of the Swedish national team that reached the final of the World Cup in 1958 and lost to Brazil. A player playing in that tournament went on to bigger and better things. His name (short version) was 'Pele'. Oh, what could have been!

Anyway, by working with age groups no younger than 17, I did not have to do reports and extinguish a young boy's dream. I was reporting on players who were already professionals and had a career. I only said not good enough for the team I was working for and would not improve our squad.

It was a small and select team of scouts, with a number being released, I found out I was the only one brought in as the 'new boy on the block'.

I was the least experienced of all the scouts and perception is reality as they say. Word soon spread that I had been brought in by Kevin, in fact I was brought in by Arthur Cox, which in truth was more of a compliment. Arthur did not suffer fools gladly, he said what he had to say and that was it. You knew when Arthur phoned you it would be short and sweet and to the point. When he had said what he had called about, he would say, "I'll speak to you shortly." You knew that was the end of the conversation and he would hang up.

Being brought in by Arthur and Kevin, people made up their own minds. In the early days whenever the scouts got together, I sensed a shade of caution as they, I am sure, thought I was getting special treatment and was only there on the back of my association with them; especially Kevin Keegan having gone to school with him.

Nothing could have been further from the truth, but even I thought there might be something in it, as I was still learning my trade. Kevin did tell me on one occasion in private that had I not come up to scratch at Fulham, he would have told me he. In fact, he did say that spotting a player and doing an opposition match report were two completely different disciplines, one was generally a one pager but, the other could be two dozen pages.

He said that I was one of the few scouts that could undertake this discipline, being used for both. I was delighted, that boosted my confidence no end.

Having worked for other managers at Fulham helped build my reputation, but I felt there was still some degree of scepticism in the early days at Manchester City, so I was still open to scrutiny to see what I was made of.

I decided that I would need to show confidence in my ability and organisational skills, having been in banking stood me in good stead, without being too pushy. However, in the early days for some reason, I emerged as the 'informal leader' whenever the scouts got together, I was the one approached by others, that picked up the bill or signed for things people just seemed attracted to me to take charge of settling things etc. I kept it low key and was mindful of the experience, especially with Willie (God bless him) and John Ferguson who had seemingly been with the club forever.

Towards the end of Kevin's reign, I still think the other scouts thought, in a nice way, that I had some pull with Kevin which in truth was not the case. In day-to-day discussions I was no different to others within the team.

With the close season coming to an end, the excitement was growing. Kevin had taken over on the 1st of July 2001 and I had joined shortly afterwards. The difference between being involved with Fulham and joining Manchester City was there for all to see, a much bigger club with immediate expectations to return to the Premiership at the first time of asking.

From the outset, I was being asked to do more, especially on the team analysis side of things. This is how it worked. The club choose to carry out three match reports on the opposition prior to playing them, with the last report obviously being the most important. Having watched the game, the report had to be turned around very quickly. For example, we could be playing Millwall on a Tuesday or a Wednesday, so the last game would be on the previous Saturday. That report had to be sent by 12 noon on the Sunday, so all the reports could be collated and merged by the analysts into one working document.

This was how tight the turnaround was, if the last game on a team was on a Tuesday or a Wednesday for a game the following Saturday that had to be in by 12 noon on the Thursday.

It soon became clear they were using me more for these reports than for player recruitment purposes.

Again, I will explain, with match report analysis you get an immediate return on what you have submitted. The pressure to get it right is full on because usually, you only do one or at most two of the three games. You must identify the strengths and weaknesses; the formation; which players lacked pace, to enable our players like Shaun Wright-Philips to exploit that weakness.

The final document could be as many as 24 pages, which included diagrams for set pieces for both offensive and defensive corners, free kicks etc. On these you had to draw a diagram and give the movement of the key players, any blocking tactics etc, any player who was the specific target for the ball and so on.

These reports became personal, in that you were playing a part that was vital in supplying the correct information to give the team an edge.

One occasion that I remember well was when I was at Fulham, they were playing Lincoln. We're long ball specialists and were particularly dangerous from long throw-ins into the box. On the day of the game I was going to the match having done reports on Lincoln (I lived in Lincoln), so this was a chance to see my team play which also helped with my understanding of our ability as a team.

On the day of the game, an hour and a half prior to kick off I saw a full back (whose name escapes me) was in the squad. He had been injured and if he played this would be his first game back and we had nothing on him.

His strength was that he could deliver at pace a long flat throw directly into the box, into the area around the six-yard box. Lincoln had lots of success from these throw-ins.

Anyway, I got a message to Kevin and told him what I thought might happen and that it was often better to give away a corner rather than a throw in.

After four or so minutes, yes you guessed it, Lincoln won a throw some 15 yards from the corner flag and yes, the player in question was playing. He took the throw in; I held my breath as the ball at pace was delivered into the six-yard box. We were ready and the defence held firm, we snuffed out the danger and gave them very few opportunities after that, we went on to win the game 2-1 with Peter Beardsley scoring both.

After the game in the lounge, Kevin came up to me put his arms around me and said, "Starzzy that information about the long throw was crucial we would have been 1-0 down after 5 minutes if you had not warned me."

It brought it home to me how important, even the smallest bit of information can make a difference, to say I was over the moon is an understatement.

Season 2001/02 - The Championship

The early work had been done the fixtures were out and our first game in the Championship was at home to Watford on the 11th August. We won it 3-0, it was a great start at Maine Road. I also had one eye on Fulham, who were now in the Premiership - had I made the right decision?

The season was underway, whilst expectations were high, Kevin had to rebuild confidence and get the new players integrated into the squad.

We, on paper, had a strong squad with many players who were and are still household names: Nicky Weaver, Stuart Pearce (Captain), Darren Huckerby, Paul Dickov, Shaun Goater, Richard Dunne, Eyal Berkovic, Paulo Wanchope, Steve Howey, Shaun Wright-Philips.

There were two other players worthy of a special mention and a story that goes with them.

But first I must mention Ali Bernabia. He turned out in my opinion to be the signing of the season. In today's terms he was the equivalent to David Silva.

Ali made us tick. His ability, his all-round touch and control was outstanding and to the best of my knowledge, he cost us nothing. He had been on trial at Sunderland who decided he was not for them (not sure who made that decision, but it was a big mistake). He was also being linked with West Ham, but Kevin stepped in and signed him.

He played 38 league games and scored eight goals, but he was more involved in setting up with 'assists' as it is termed today. Kevin said after that season that he wishes he had had him 10 years earlier as he was one of the best players he had ever worked with.

The other noteworthy player was Christian Negouai. Christian was a young, strong boy recommended to Kevin by Phillipe Albert; an outstanding centre half who had played for Kevin at Newcastle United.

By chance I was up in Manchester at the training ground at Carrington. Christian was there on trial. I was asked to watch him over a couple of days and then sit in on the discussion as to whether he would be signed or not. He showed great enthusiasm and was prepared to put a foot in (without doubt). He also possessed a good work rate and attitude.

He was asked to participate in a defence versus attack session, where he played his part as a defensive midfielder closing down on attacking players who had to weave in and out of slalom like posts with the ball then get a shot away before being tackled by the defender. The defender, on a whistle, had to head the ball three times back to a thrower then close down the attacker.

To say he made his 'mark' is an understatement. Darren Huckerby was the next to go on the whistle, coming through the posts and it was Christian's job to close him down as quickly as possible. Darren was just emerging from the final slalom pole when Christian clattered him full on, Darren ended up on his back holding his leg, Christian had well and truly done his job. Kevin told Darren to get up and stop milking it. However, Darren was not amused, "Gaffer I am injured" he replied

Kevin responded, "Get up you *****"

Until he got close to Darren and saw blood coming from his leg.

An "Oh" followed from Kevin.

It transpired that Darren needed stitches and missed the next few games.

The next session was a defence versus attack game with Carlo Nash and Nicky Weaver taking it in turn to play in goal.

Christian was told to take things a little easier, no need to try too hard to impress.

To say this fell on deaf ears is also an understatement, he tackled with gusto and no holding back. I was standing behind the goal near Nicky and Carlo.

Christian was taking players out left right and centre the final straw came when he not only clattered Eyal Berkovich who was not amused at all then moved on to Ali Bernabia who managed to avoid his challenge.

Both Nicky and Carlo turned to me and said, "If we don't stop this session now, we will need to sign him as we will have no other players left."

It was now time for the discussion, there was no doubting he was a destructive defensive minded player. He would make a great number six as they say, he was committed but could not be as rash in his challenges. We all agreed he was probably trying too hard... how wrong we all were.

The decision was made to sign him and develop him into the holding number six. Unfortunately, he was not the most intelligent person and struggled to take and retain instructions.

On one occasion he was scheduled to take a regular drugs test when he arrived for training, with the test to be carried out as soon as training had finished. Christian trained and went back into the dressing room as usual.

Shortly afterwards, he was required to undertake the normal routine test but could not be found, until the security guard on the gate reported that he had seen him leave the training complex a little while earlier, it transpired that he had gone to the airport at Manchester to collect a family member who was travelling in from Belgium and thought they would just wait till he got back.

He did not appreciate the ramifications of his actions, he was not trying to miss or be devious about the test, he just failed to prioritise his actions by even just telling someone. In the end, he took the test later that day and was given the all clear. The situation had been sorted and no harm was done.

On another occasion he was living in rented accommodation which had rules and regulations. He was told that he could not have pets. All was fine for a while then one day he was called into the office to explain something.

He was asked "Why have you got pets?"

"I don't have pets" he replied.

He was challenged and was told he had been seen with a dog,

"Oh yes I have a dog" he said.

"So, you do have pets"

"No, I only have one dog" was his riposte

He had assumed pets was in the plural, so it was all right to have one dog!

That explains a lot, but a genuine lad who should have done more in football - a talent unfulfilled.

On his debut he had to be substituted after picking up a yellow card as it was only a matter of time before he would pick up a second and therefore see a red.

It transpired that he only made two appearances. To be fair to him, mainly due to the exuberance and enthusiasm which he found difficult to control, and no amount of coaching was going to change him as he played the way he played and that was that. Real shame because he could have been a great holding player.

Christian was also hampered by injury in his career with Manchester City and in total played only two games in that first season and six appearances in total for the first team. He did in fact cost around £1.5 million from Charleroi in Belgium. In total, he spent five years at Manchester City being more of a success in the reserves but could have done much more. Not a great start to my recommendations to sign a player but at least I was not alone with all others Kevin, Arthur etc, saying basically the same.

We had started well in the Championship winning our first game 3-0 but with 45 games more to play it was going to be a long hard season.

As I said previously, scouts take as much pleasure, if not more, doing match reports which deliver an immediate return on the work undertaken. Often with player reports / assessments it can take forever to sign a player that you have suggested and at times you may not sign them at all, often other clubs get there first, or they're going to cost too much money. This can be very frustrating but as a scout you soon learn to accept it and move on to the next one.

For example, I mentioned Shaun Wright-Philips to Fulham just before I left for Manchester City. I was glad he never left City, as he became a great player for us, and we eventually sold him to Chelsea for a fee in excess of £20 million.

A few other players that I mentioned for Manchester City at this time were Matthew Etherington and Michael Dawson who both went to spurs. I was particularly keen on Dawson whom I had seen as a youngster playing in the reserves, he just stood out and predicted that he would not only play for England he would make a good captain. He suffered from glandular fever not long after that recommendation which held him back. However, he did play at the highest level, so in the long run I was proved right. It does not always work out that way.

On the other side of the coin people often ask, who is the best player you have found.

I start the reply by saying you don't find many who are not known these days because of the extensive coverage on television with Sky etc. It's more of 'can do a job' and 'are they going to improve the squad'. What I do say though, it's not often who you recommend and sign, it's just as important who you keep away from the club by being positive and decisive in your report. For example, Arthur Cox rang me and said, "I know this is a big ask but could you go to Germany at the weekend to watch a player playing for Schalke away at Hertha Berlin, he was a Belgian international".

Arthur said we are very keen on him and they want a fee of £6 to £8 million. Kevin and I want your opinion before we proceed, at that time that was big money for Manchester City to spend on one player.

Everything was arranged. Manchester City sorted everything for you; your flight, ticket, hotel etc the same happens for games in the UK except change flight to parking if possible.

I was off on my first ever scouting trip abroad which sound's glamorous (at first) but soon you realize it's not fun getting a 6am flight, having to leave home before 3am to check in, get to the hotel check in get to the ground and try to make yourself understood in a foreign language.

Everything went well, I was at the ground, all I needed was a team sheet to see if he was playing; getting an official team sheet proved difficult but eventually I did get one. Yes, he was playing, in future visits abroad that was not always the case. Sometimes you travel abroad to watch a specific player who is not in the squad, a total waste of time! Again, you get used to it happening, I have been to Poland, Serbia, Romania etc and no player to watch, so you come home, as planned, with nothing to report.

Anyway, on this first occasion he is playing. I am conscious that we appear to be on the verge of signing him, but Arthur's voice is in my head.

"You write what you see, not what you want to see based on other people's comments or opinions."

In short, he was a shocker, he lacked energy, enthusiasm, attitude and all-round ability on the day. He was substituted on 62 minutes.

I now had to write a report, bearing in mind I had been sent because others had recommended him, and we were apparently close to signing him. What do I do water it down? - No I went for it and wrote that, 'I would not touch him with a barge pole'. Then gave my analysis and assessment as to why I did not like him.

We never signed him following that report, he went to United Arab Emirates, Qatar, I think, he disappeared from the European scene and probably picked up a big pay day. I had been proved correct; he never did much after that. However, we did end up signing him some years later as a free agent, on a one-year deal. He was released after one year. He never tried a lot until the last few months of his contract, probably to get a new deal (that's what I thought anyway). I feel I was vindicated. I had not been influenced by the comments prior to my trip to Berlin. I have continued to do reports on the same basis ever since, too many scouts in my opinion sit on the fence and will not decide. I will explain how players are assessed in due course when it will become clear.

To our season in the Championship on the pitch, we started well and got better and better.

	Manchester City overall	Matches involved with scouting
Played	46	35
Won	31	28
Drew	6	5
Lost	9	2
Goal difference	+56	
Points	99	89
Win ratio	67	80

As you can see from the statistics, we had a great record, and this resulted in us achieving promotion at the first time of asking. We finished 10 points ahead of second placed West Bromwich Albion; which made our last game of the season at Maine Road such an enjoyable occasion. We won the game 3-1 against Portsmouth and achieved a record attendance of 34,657.

From a personal perspective, you can see my statistics for the teams I scouted in the build-up to a game, in comparison to the overall results above. To say I was delighted with the end result is a huge understatement!

That final game was fun to be at. It became a tradition that the scouts and their wives would be invited to the final home game of the season. We would be put up in a hotel for two nights, on this occasion it was the Midland in Manchester, transported to the game and given the VIP treatment. This was something Kevin and Arthur started and became a recurring theme. We were wined and dined prior to the game and taken to the pitch for a photo opportunity with the management team.

As I said previously, I had become the informal leader as the season had progressed, with Kevin taking the mickey out of me from time to time and setting me up. He also on occasion would single me out and give me instructions to sort things out. This only enhanced my reputation within the scouts, who now also used to ask me to sort things for them, like getting photos of them with the trophy. I had become the focus and organiser.

Prior to the game as I mentioned we were entertained before being taken to Kevin's private lounge before kick-off. He had a fridge in the room, which was located in the tunnel area. He said "go and take everyone into my room and help yourselves to a beer etc from the fridge I will be with you shortly." He came into his lounge after about 10 minutes, I had a beer in my hand and he quickly said "Starzzy you drank all my beer", the other scouts were quickly trying to hide theirs behind their backs.

He was joking of course, he then said to me "Starzzy take everyone onto the pitch to the centre circle". I led everyone out of his room down the tunnel and onto the side of the pitch, Kevin held back. As I walked onto the pitch, I got 3 or 4 yards from the touchline,

"Where do you think you're going?" a security guard shouted,

"Kevin Keegan told me to take the scouting party to the centre circle." I said

"Did I, I don't remember that?" Said a smirking Kevin Keegan, the other scouts were laughing that yet again he had set me up. This was not the first, or last time he embarrassed me - he did it regularly when we were together.

Returning to the game it was a party atmosphere, already crowned champions but wanting to finish off in style. The game was really a non-event with us winning comfortably 3-1. With goals from Steve Howey, Shaun 'Feed the Goat' Goater and last, but not least, Jon Macken.

Also, on that day it was Stuart Pearce's last game before retiring he was on 99 goals for his career and everybody wanted him to get his 100 to finish what had been a great career, what a great way to finish off. There was nothing at stake for either side that could affect others so in the last 10 minutes or so, Stuart was pushed higher and higher to try and get that 100th goal. His shots were either saved or whistled wide of the goal, the more he tried the harder it seemed to be to get a shot on target.

The referee played in total nearly 12 minutes of injury time to try and help Stuart get that elusive goal. Despite attempt after attempt still no goal until a Portsmouth player deliberately stuck a handout to give a penalty away. Surely this was it. Fitting given Stuart's history with penalties that he should finish his career scoring his 100th goal from the spot.

Dave Beasant was the keeper, as Stuart picked up the ball to place it on the spot, Dave walked towards him and said something to him before walking back to the goal line. Stuart did his usual and decided to blast the ball as hard as he could. The crowd were in raptures what a way to not only finish a glittering career to get his 100th goal but score what would have I believe been a record 109th goal in a season. The crowd were waiting to cheer and salute Stuart. Expectations were at fever pitch. Stuart started his run up, the crowd getting louder and louder. Stuart struck the ball with a fierce right foot high, but unfortunately wide of Dave Beasant's right hand post. The crowd were devastated, the referee had to blow the final whistle it all became a big anti-climax.

I was in the tunnel area shortly after the game had finished to overhear a conversation between Dave Beasant and some others, saying that when he walked towards Stuart prior to the penalty kick being taken, he had told him to place the ball to his left as he was going to dive to his right.

However, Stuart being Stuart, he wanted to go out in style with a typical full-blooded strike he was going to burst the net and do his customary celebration. It was just not meant to be!

That evening, a party had been arranged for all players and staff in the Midland Hotel with a free bar, food and entertainment. What a great night it was! Again, my informal leader tag came to the fore. Some scouts wanted pictures with Kevin and the trophy, but they were too scared to ask him personally, so I was asked to arrange it with him. Suffice to say Kevin was only too pleased to oblige and many if not all scouts including Lynda and myself had pictures taken.

As the evening rolled on and the drink was flowing Lynda and I got chatting to Kevin's wife Jean and her two daughters, whom we knew.

"Do you have a drink?" I asked,

"No" they replied.

"Can you get us three Sambuca's?" Lynda said, "I'll have one as well".

So, off I trudge to get the drinks from the free bar, only to be advised that the free bar had just closed and therefore I had to pay. Just my luck free bar all night and I get stung for 4 Sambuca's!

Kevin could not stop laughing then said, "you can always put it on your expenses, as Arthur will think it's an Argentinian centre forward." At that point everybody just burst out laughing at my expense, needless to say I did not claim the Sambuca's back on my expenses, Kevin has never let me forget it.

One last short story from that season. With the season going well Kevin and co decided to take out some insurance in the January transfer window and buy Jon Macken, a striker and prolific goal scorer from Preston, for £5 million.

Unfortunately, he suffered from many injuries following his transfer and only made 27 starts and 51 appearances in total scoring only 7 during his 3-year period at Manchester City.

Whilst I was at Carrington training ground on a visit, Kevin took me and gave me a tour of some of the facilities. One area was a new rehabilitation pool. We went into the building and Jon Macken was in the pool with a medical supervisor putting him through his paces. What it entails is to walk in water up to your waist against the tide with pressure being increased as you walk in the water, which supports his knees which is what he was doing for physio treatment.

Kevin asked the physio to increase the pressure, which was at the minimum, to show us how it works, Kevin repeated this request a few times till we were at maximum pressure.

Macken started off at the top of the pool quite comfortably but as the pressure in the tank increased, he was gradually carried towards the back of the pool. Jon Macken's face was a picture the more the pressure was being increased the further back he went, by the time he was nearly at the back of the pool Kevin said "you had better close it down." By now he was nearly at the very end of the pool, Kevin said "God! I paid £5 million for him and he is either going to drown or end up in the car park!"

As the machine was turned off, Jon Macken was relieved. His face spoke a thousand words. Every time he saw me after that he gave me some funny looks, as if it triggered a bad memory.

Macken never really recovered from his injuries and although scoring in the final game against Portsmouth in that 3-1 win on the final day of the season, he only played 4 games in that season. His career basically stalled, and he was never the same player.

With the Championship well and truly won we needed to prepare for the return to the Premiership in season 2002/03.

6

LIFE IN THE PREMIERSHIP

Season 2002/03

This time I was staying where I was. Having won the title with Manchester City, could things get any better? I was part of the team albeit on a part time basis and on a small retainer, plus expenses that had won the Championship again, having already won it with Fulham under Jean Tigana.

This was going to be the toughest season yet, being in the Premiership. Fulham had finished 14th in their first season back, we were now joining them and hoped to do better, although we had seen how tough it was for Fulham. I had learnt a lot since that first scouting trip and my learning curve was not flattening, in fact over the coming years, it got steeper and steeper as the club grew in stature and I was still learning some 18 years later when I retired.

By now I had retired from National Westminster Bank due to a heart attack, the actual dates are a blur, but I remember the events that led up to me retiring from my main source of income.

Coming back from Grimsby where I held our usual monthly meeting with my sales team. I was driving and speaking on the phone (hands free of course) to Mark Briggs one of my best financial advisers. When nearing the ring road on the way into Lincoln I suffered a very sharp pain in my chest on the left side which left me taking a sharp intake of breath. I gasped, "Are you OK?" Mark said,

"I'm not sure." I replied

I was only 49 going on 50, this may sound a bit morbid, but I do remember that I had always predicted, for many years, that I would not see 50. The reason for this somewhat macabre prediction is revealed in the NWB - The Playing Years Story.

I had a choice to make but the pain subsided after 100 yards or so I thought I was ok; I'll just go back to the office. As I approached the roundabout, I had another shooting pain, so I either went left to the hospital or right to the office, the pain was not totally gone so I went left to the hospital (the best decision I ever made!) I got to the hospital car park, tried to get out of my car and my legs would not work. I eventually managed to get into the A & E reception and I was taken in right away on a trolley. at this point I did not know what had happened.

We needed to strengthen the squad, and whilst I had no input into the eventual signings, I did report on players and give an opinion on whether they were good enough or not to improve our squad. I was still doing the job.

Reports were getting more and more complicated and detailed. We had a system called "Scout 7" which was a standardised reporting template that has many pages and was the basis for the reports, not only player assessments which were normally one page but for match reports on the opposition which would be at least 20 pages. All of these are regularly updated changed to reflect what information is required, so you must keep up with your understanding.

The conclusion in respect of a player report came down to one of four marks based on your opinion on that player. Initially the reports were free format but now that has changed to a template that is position specific, but the final marking has remained constant.

In that first season back in the Premiership the player reports were in the free format with a mark given as follows.

D - means he is not good enough to add to our squad

C - means he has some quality but needs to be assessed against others as and when but unlikely to be suitable

B - means he should be looked at very closely as a potential target as soon as possible by me and by others

A - means he is top drawer top quality and sign him. (You don't get many of them.)

Kevin had also added a section/template headed "How do we beat the opposition?"

Basically, you had to summarise your report and be specific in a few sentences on their strengths and weaknesses. No easy task for teams like Arsenal.

I jokingly mentioned in my report on Arsenal, prior to the game at Maine Road on the 22nd Feb 2003 having already lost away to them 2-1 in September 2002, that the only weakness I could find was that "The air conditioning on the team bus was faulty".

I did of course put the real weaknesses down and my joke was taken in good spirit. We lost at home 1-5. So, perhaps I was right after all.

As the years went on, finding a rated player for the first team got harder and harder. But in my opinion too many scouts sit on the fence and give a 'C', I felt it to be a kop out.

A couple of seasons ago, tongue-in-cheek, I was given an award at a global scout's meeting I received a cup for the most consistent scout for reports submitted. The award was for the fact that I had given 98% player reports as 'D'. But the point was made that if I gave players a mark of 'B' or, God forbid an 'A', which were and still are as rare as rocking horse s***, word goes around the scouting and recruitment office and people take notice.

I had a reputation for being precise and that stemmed from my early days. For example, I said to buy John Stones, after watching him play for Barnsley against Leeds, as a full back (one report) but I said he is a centre back who can play as a number 6 (holding player) he would have cost around £3 million. Less than two years later we paid in excess of £50 million!

I thought we had made some very good signings and the squad looked stronger. We signed players such as Nicolas Anelka for a club record fee of £13 million. Sylvain Distin a strong centre back and leader who turned out to be a bargain at £5 million. A big surprise in Peter Schmeichel but again a good solid signing. I must mention Marc Vivien Foe signed from PSG and in the January, Robbie Fowler. We already had players such as Shaun Wright-Phillips who was making his mark, Danny Tiato, Ali Bernabia, who everyone was now impressed with, Sun Jihai and Eyal Berkovic to name but a few.

Oh, and I forgot a young guy coming through from the academy, Joey Barton was in the squad. He became a regular and a bit of a rebel on the pitch. He was competitive and uncompromising, I met him once at Everton in the directors' box, a nicer guy you could not wish to meet. We were ready to go.

The season was not going to be like the previous season where we had broken many club records in winning the Championship and regaining our place in the Premiership, but we were confident as a team that we could more than hold our own.

In fact, we finished ninth and Fulham who's results I always looked for finished 14th again. We had beaten them both home and away 4-1 at home and 1-0 away, both teams were back in the Premiership together, but it looked as if I had made the right choice to join Manchester City.

The main results as far as the fans were concerned was the fact that we had beaten United 3-1 at home and drawn 1-1 away.

This was to be our last season playing at Maine Road before moving next season to our new home the City of Manchester Stadium (now renamed 'the Etihad' under corporate sponsorship a few years later which is another story).

Marc Vivien Foe scored the last goal at Maine Road on the 21st April 2003, in a 3-0 victory over Sunderland.

Marc sadly died aged 28 whilst on international duty on 26th June 2003. Kevin retired his shirt number 23, never to be worn again and Lyon also retired his number 17. A talent gone too soon.

We had finished ninth but qualified for the following season's UEFA cup as Fair Play winners, little did I know what part I was about to play in that European and future European campaigns.

Happy Birthday to me!

One area of disappointment was our exit from the League Cup away at Wigan, a lower league club on the 5th November 2002. That was my birthday and the big 5-O.

Unbeknown to me Lynda had been in contact with Julia, Kevin's personal assistant who had been liaising with Kevin to give me a surprise. Suddenly, on the morning of 4th November Lynda said "pack your bag you are going to Manchester City!"

"What for?" I asked,

"Kevin has invited you up for your birthday." she replied

So, I packed a bag and headed off to the training ground. I arrived in time for lunch and afternoon training, I was kitted out with gear and boots etc.

I recall after a light training session Kevin kept Shaun Wright-Phillips back for some extra work that I got involved with. He was trying to get Shaun to be more positive and deliver balls to the back-post area. I was tasked with delivering balls into Kevin's feet for him to set up crosses from the right by Shaun to the back post with a first-time delivery.

I remember Kevin saying, "What I want Shaun, is for you to run onto the ball down the right flank near the penalty area and aim for the back post, let me show you."

I played the ball into the area that Kevin ran onto and right footed he delivered a pinpoint cross, hitting the back post near the crossbar.

He turned to Shaun and said, "There you go it's easy!"

Shaun looked at me and I looked back at him in disbelief and amazement.

As Shaun took up position to have a go, I said to Kevin "You've still got it."

"Yes," he replied, "but I won't be having another go, that's the first time I have managed to hit the post!" He smiled and worked with Shaun on delivery and technique. Shaun did well Kevin had given him the confidence to be positive. I watched him take this into games on a regular basis, together with other areas of his game that he had worked on with Kevin during that season. Kevin had improved him as a player.

He was sold later for around £20 million to Chelsea but never hit the heights he had achieved at Manchester City. He did return to Manchester City but was not the same player. In my opinion he owed Kevin a lot for spending time with him, a nice lad.

Once training was over, we showered and went to Kevin's office for a meeting before going to the hotel me, Kevin, Stuart Pearce and Arthur were all staying in the same hotel (Manchester City picking up my bill).

We were all going to watch the reserves play at Hyde United's ground, Kevin said he would drive to the training ground and I left my car at Carrington. Kevin said to be downstairs in half an hour, so as we have plenty of time to get to Hyde.

I rushed and got changed, was downstairs in less than 25 min to see Arthur Cox and Stuart Pearce eating sandwiches from a large silver plate.

Stuart said "Starrzy (he was now calling me that) help yourself". There were only about four left so I dug in, I was starving, "there is only one left you might as well eat it."

As I picked up the final sandwich Kevin arrived, I had half the sandwich in my mouth so could not speak

"Where are the sandwiches I ordered?" Kevin asked,

"Starrzy's eaten them" Stuart replied, as quick as a flash. My mouth was full Kevin knew I had been set up but told everyone we met that night " You invite a guy up for his birthday and he eats your sandwiches."

Stuart could not stop laughing.

We arrived at Hyde it was a cold dank night, as we walked from the car, I was next to Kevin we are of similar height and by now hair colour. A fan came from behind us tapped me on the shoulder and said, "Kevin can I have your autograph?" Kevin turned and the guy said, "Oh sorry I thought that he was you," pointing to me.

Kevin signed the guy's book turned to us all and said, "Bloody hell if I am starting to look like you Starrzy I have got problems".

He went on to say, "But it's not all bad I might put you in the dugout and if things are not going well, I can send you out to the technical area and take the abuse", everyone laughed.

The next day I checked out of the hotel and Kevin drove me to the training ground where I again got into some gear and watched training. When training finished, we got dressed and headed for the restaurant on the upper floor, by now the players were coming in for lunch. The whole place was full of players, staff etc. Suddenly out of my left eye, I spotted a chef carrying a birthday cake with candles fully alight. At this point Richard Dunne stood up and exclaimed, in a jovial manner " Why has he got a large cake when I only got a small one?"

Kevin quick as a flash replied, "Because he is more valuable and important than you, defenders are ten a penny, first class scouts are hard to come by." The other players laughed Richard sat down smiling, I sat there embarrassed but proud.

We got ready to go to the game I got my car ready, Kevin said "leave your car, we will come back here after the game, so you can pick it up then and head for home." I was ushered onto the team bus, got pride of place on the front seat next to Kevin and we headed for Wigan. I was treated like part of the staff being in the dressing room prior to kick off, listening to the team talk etc.

Everything had gone well up to that point, I could not have asked for more from my 50th. It was a birthday I was always going to remember (although Lynda had another surprise lined up).

However, Wigan were to spoil the party, they were going well in what is now known as League One they beat us 1-0.

Kevin said on the way home on the bus, "That's the last time you come and watch, you are bad luck", he was kidding of course but he had to blame somebody.

As the league campaign continued, we held our own and finished 9th with 51 points with the title going to United with a total of 83 points.

Oh, how things have changed.

We were now looking forward to next season but, Kevin's ally in the boardroom David Bernstein had left the club so things were going to change on several fronts.

The News That Surprised Me

I mentioned earlier about the pain in my chest on the way back from Grimsby and making the best decision to go to hospital, I was referred to my GP, who referred me to Dr Andrews a private cardiologist, I had private health cover through NatWest Bank.

I had been working normally since the first episode and felt all right. When I saw Dr Andrews for the first time, I was expecting him to say I drank too much, I was overweight and was suffering from stress. By this time, I was an Area Manager in regulated sales in NatWest life, managing a team of financial advisers.

Dr Andrews informed me that I needed to undergo some tests, one being an angiogram.

He then told me from what he'd seen so far, I'd had a heart attack and therefore I would not be going back to work until I had completed all the appropriate tests.

He could see by my face that I was surprised and said to me.

"You were not expecting that were you?" I wasn't and mentioned the weight stress etc.

As I was a private patient I was seen very quickly. An appointment was arranged for an overnight stay in Nottingham BMI hospital for the tests.

In the meantime, I would not be going back to work until he said so. I left his office with Lynda, both in some degree of shock and disbelief. I was only 49!

We parked up in Tesco's car park, I had a car phone, and I do not know why but I said to Lynda

"When I call my manager say nothing, so as not to let her know you are in the car."

I dialled the number and she answered I told her I had some bad news, that my cardiologist Dr Andrews wanted me to undergo some tests and had signed me off from work with immediate effect.

I had worked for NatWest since 1970, I was NatWest through and through, cut me in half and like a stick of rock you would have found NWB running through me.

But what happened next killed a part of me that has never recovered.

After a short pregnant pause, she said "Did you know that one of my advisers, who had been off with stress, was returning to work today?"

"Yes", I replied, what she said next I will never forget,

"Can you drive over to see him (about an hour and a half drive each way) before you go off sick?"

There was no sympathy for the news I had just received, no comment, or no I am sorry to hear that, nothing!

A part of me died in that moment, I could see Lynda was furious and I had to cover her mouth to stop her from verbally tearing her head off.

I replied to her in a strong firm voice "No I can't! - doctors' orders - until I have undergone the tests."

So, I was officially off work, I went to Nottingham for the tests a few days later. Having had the tests, Dr Andrews came to see me the next morning in hospital.

He stood at the bottom of my bed and on reflection he was checking what I was like, he said "What is it you do?" I explained both roles, he then asked if I enjoyed the bank role, "I used to" I said "but it's harder and harder with targets etc, the football is not a job, just a hobby, in fact it takes my mind off the bank job at weekends."

We then had a general discussion, he then asked me if I wanted the good news or the bad news!

I opted for the good news, he told me that your arteries are like roads, you have major roads like 'A' roads and 'B' roads. He told me my main roads were generally all right. It was my 'B' roads that are the problem, and there is nothing I can do on a surgical basis so that's the bad news. But we can try to stabilise your condition with medication.

I was confused and shocked. He asked me again about my bank role.

He then came out with the following. "What if I said you won't be going back to work? You will never go back." The look on my face must have been a picture.

I said "Royal Bank of Scotland will have something to say about that."

He replied, "They will not dare to obstruct me or refuse to carry out my instructions!"

I was shocked to say the least, but he was so confident in his decision I was in shock again. Things were happening at a furious pace.

I was discharged from hospital and started to prepare for what was to happen next. The rest is history as they say, I was on long term sick getting full pay for a while. Then one day I was advised I was to be retired on ill health grounds. I had done over 37 years' service with NatWest and to be fair to my line manager, she did obtain a full-service pension for me.

I had looked at my situation some time previously (seven years or so ago) and sold myself income protection to cover any shortfall in my income for such an eventuality. I was now in a position to make a claim.

Whilst I did not wish to ever claim on the policy, I would be no worse off financially for years to come. As a financial advisor I was expected to give people good advice and so I had followed this path for myself and it paid off.

I continue to see Dr Andrews on an annual basis, just for a check-up which is money well spent, as I found out soon after.

On my regular visit he told me the situation regarding my heart is fine, however he thought I may be in the early stages of Parkinson's.

He was going to refer me to an appropriate consultant. I contacted Manchester City to see if I was covered as part of my package, which included private health cover and I was.

I had used the private health cover previously to have an operation on my left knee which was the one I injured many years ago playing for NatWest.

I was referred to a Professor Sharma, a specialist in dealing with Parkinson's. Whilst he was assessing me, I mentioned that I'd noticed over recent years that I was becoming increasingly hard of hearing in my right ear. He arranged for an MRI scan (again paid for by MCFC).

Again, the right decision. They found that I had a benign tumour on my brain which was putting pressure on my hearing and I was diagnosed with an acoustic neuroma.

I was referred to a neurologist Professor Kenemey in Sheffield. Again, MCFC picked up the bill. I had to undergo some more scans and go back for the results; this was around March 2016.

When I went back to see Professor Kenemey he sat me down and told me there were three options we can take.

We can perform open brain surgery, but I do not recommend that, because of your heart condition and as you are on Warfarin you would die on the operating table.

I hoped the next two options are better than the first.

Do nothing and I would probably be all right for 10 years or so, but eventually the tumour would grow and put increased pressure on the brain and that would kill me!

Better but still not satisfactory.

The final solution is to have a relatively new procedure where they blast the tumour with 192 rays of radiation (don't know why its 192). He went on to explain what was required they scan the brain, pinpoint the area affected by the tumour, blast it for 35-40 minutes with the radiation beams whilst my head is trapped in a vice so I can't move.

"What happens if you miss?" I asked,

"We don't" he replied,

"Yes, but what if you do?" I repeated,

"We don't," he retorted, "but if we did you would die."

I wish I had not asked. He said that they had a good success rate of around 90%. I decided that's the one for me then. The procedure was agreed I contacted MCFC to see if I was covered as this was going to be a privately funded procedure not available on the NHS. MCFC confirmed I could proceed along with future consultations.

Professor Kenemey said they were looking to stop the growth by cauterising the tumour, anything else would be a bonus.

All went well but I had to wait 12 months for the results.

In the meantime, the bill had to be paid for the procedure and treatment. To my horror the bill came to over £19,000.

12 months later, I had more scans and found that not only had the tumour not got any bigger, it had actually reduced.

Professor Kenemey said that whilst he couldn't be certain, the kick on the head I got playing for the bank all those years ago, which resulted in a detached retina, may well have been dormant for many years and I knew nothing about it until now.

How lucky was I? MCFC were great and picked up every bill!

My most recent visit was in April 2019 and I have been told it is under control.

Lincoln City v Manchester City (29th July 2003)

Towards the end of Kevin's reign, my son Paul was at university in Sheffield. He was a Lincoln City supporter through and through (and still is) and he phoned me to say it looked like Lincoln were virtually broke and on the verge of going out of business.

He asked if I could do him a favour, would I ring Kevin and ask him to bring the Manchester City first team down to Lincoln for a pre-season friendly, to raise some cash to help Lincoln stave off administration or worse.

I told him he had to be joking but Paul passionately replied that they were going out of business and need the promise of money etc. Well what could I do? - I fabricated a reason to call Kevin, I mentioned to him that Paul had been on the phone asking if we could help. I said it was a tall ask but to my surprise Kevin told me to get the Lincoln chairman, Rob Bradley, to ring him or get his number and he would see what he could do.

To cut a long story very short they managed to speak and sorted something out. Manchester City brought a full first team down for a game on a Tuesday night. They virtually sold out and raised in the region of £50,000+, which kept Lincoln City afloat. Manchester City did not even take expenses and Lincoln kept all the proceeds. So, perhaps I did have a degree of pull after all!

Season 2003/04

Season 2003/04 was soon upon us and with the added aspect of

European football it was going to be a searching and tough season.

In truth, it was a difficult season all round and European football and a new stadium nearly brought about our downfall. We finished 16th of 18 but with only one team going down (Leicester) as the number of teams was restructured, we were safe for another year.

We had added to the squad with David James in goal, Claudio Reyna, Steve McManaman, along with a few others. I was learning the scouting role from a new perspective in a team that was struggling, I was not getting the results from match reports that I had done previously.

I remember this season for a few reasons, firstly was for that friendly I arranged with Kevin against Lincoln City at Sincil Bank.

Secondly, there was another friendly, away at Mansfield, managed by Keith Curle. I attended and prior to the kick-off went on to the pitch with Kevin and Arthur.

The players were now warming up around us. Kevin asked Shaun to come over. Shaun made his way towards us. "I am leaving you out today son." Shaun looked amazed and a little shocked, he asked why and Kevin replied, "Well I have looked at the pitch and the grass is too long, we'll never find you."

As he turned to go back to his warmup Kevin said,

"Can I introduce you to Starrzy, one of our scouts, he's responsible for the information I use to brief the team etc".

Shaun said he was pleased to meet me, Kevin told me that Shaun's wife has just had their first baby that week. As I congratulated him, he was full of smiles.

Kevin joked "Yes, and the baby is taller than him already." He laughed and went on his way back to his warmup.

What it told me was that Kevin had a good rapport with his players and he was well liked and could have a laugh at their expense.

The only other memorable game or incident was the comeback at Spurs in the cup 3-0 down at half time, Joey Barton sent off in the tunnel at half time, something that Kevin Keegan and Faz knew nothing about. At half time, Kevin told me later he had said to Faz that they had better start queuing in the morning at the job centre. They went on to win the game 4-3 with Jon Macken getting a late winner. Their jobs were safe.

We were glad to get to the end of our first season at the City of Manchester Stadium and still be in the Premiership.

Look at the State of Him Now

As usual under Kevin, all scouts were invited up to Manchester for the last game of the season, this time against Everton. We were transported from the Worsley Park Hotel to the stadium in the official team bus. God knows how the team got there.

It must have confused the fans as we arrived at the stadium with 'Manchester City FC Team Bus' on the front.

Some were waving quite vigorously, then as they looked closer at the occupants of the coach stopped and had confused looks on their faces.

It was a typical Kevin idea to make the scouts and their wives feel special. Anyway, we had lunch then down to Kevin's room in the tunnel, waiting to go on the pitch for the customary photo.

As we finished to go to our seats, he said to me "After the game, come down and wait in my room for me and help yourselves to the drinks in the fridge." I had been caught like this before

"Yes right" I said with a sceptical tone,

"No, I mean it." He insisted.

At the end of the game, which we won 5-1, Rooney's last game for Everton before joining the other team known as M********* United (only joking).

I arranged everyone and we headed for the tunnel to Kevin's room. The tunnel area as always was packed with players, press, players' wives, you name it - including Sky's cameras.

Kevin came into his room and to my surprise he did not try to stitch me up, However, he looked a shade down. When asked why, he said,

"We have just played really well and won 5-1. Why could we not have done that all season?"

As usual he sought perfection and the result meant very little to him, hence the need to push on in the summer and not just consolidate.

We were now ready to get back onto the team bus, so one by one we left his room, as the scouts and their respective partners left his room, into the hustle and bustle of the tunnel area, Kevin kissed all the wives on the cheek and shook all the scout's hands. We were the last to leave his room.

Lynda was just ahead of me and Kevin gave her an extra big peck on the cheek as obviously we knew him well, as I came out of the room into the tunnel area, Kevin came towards me and put his arms around me.

"I am not going to kiss you" I joked. He stopped and suddenly said in a loud voice,

"Excuse me ladies and gentlemen can I just introduce Starrzy, one of our scouts, but we also went to school together" I was taken by surprise. He went on to say, "He is four years older than me!"

I am in fact 18 months younger. By this time, he had his arm round my shoulder keeping me close.

"Starrzy was a player with a lot of talent, but never got the breaks."

By now everyone from Sky to players were listening to Kevin. He continued,

"You should have seen him in his best days with pace to burn, a good athlete."

Then he hit me with the sucker punch, he held me close and tight placed his right hand on my expanded waistline and midriff and shouted very loudly as he patted it,

"And look at the state of him now"

Everyone laughed, I could not help but join in, as he said,

"You will never get the better of me!"

He gave me a big hug just to show everyone we could have a joke together.

French Restaurant

Julia, the manager's PA, was responsible for arranging the Scouts end of season get togethers.

On one occasion, when we were invited up for the last game of the season at home. At that time, the club did not have the money (we have now) and would only pay for one night's accommodation at the Midland Hotel in Manchester. Julia decided she would book a table at the exclusive French Restaurant within the Midland Hotel as we had to pay for the extra night in the Hotel ourselves.

The Scouts and their wives I seem to recall was a party of eight. As we entered the restaurant, who was sitting at the next table but Derek Fazakerley (Faz) and his party of four.

He said to me "What are you doing in here?"

At this point I did not appreciate how expensive this restaurant was.

Faz said, "Can I put my bill onto your tab?"

I replied, "No, you can't." or words to that effect and smiled.

We sat down and started looking at the menu, I looked at a few other Scouts in disbelief at the prices, but decided to just enjoy ourselves, I seem to recall that Rod Cousins and I had the Chateau Briand very expensive for two people.

We had a great evening at Manchester City's expense, and it was time to pay the bill, when it came and was passed to me again being the informal leader.

The bill came close to £800 with wine that Julia had arranged. It would have been cheaper for the club to have paid for the extra night accommodation.

A good night was had by all. Thanks to Julia.

Season - 2004/05

The season was steady and we finished 8th but a long way behind record breakers Chelsea, who won the title for the first time in 50 years. It was obvious to all and especially Kevin that we were doing well but had stalled in our progress. The team needed some investment in players and with everything else seemingly going fine

Kevin looked to strengthen the squad to move to the next level.

However, the money needed was not forthcoming and I felt Kevin was getting frustrated, when the phrase we need consolidation was thrown into the mix by the board etc., I knew Kevin was not a man to accept second best and again it was obvious to all, especially him that he had taken the club as far as he could take them.

I don't know the actual ins and outs of the discussions prior to his resignation. With the club safe I think part of the deal was that he would not wait to run out his contract or receive a payoff (which is the norm), providing Stuart Pearce was given the job, albeit on a temporary basis, with a view to a full-time appointment.

Kevin left on good terms on the 11th March 2005 and Stuart was given the caretaker job on the 12th March he was subsequently appointed as the full-time manager on the 11th May. I was not concerned about my situation as I knew Stuart quite well and thought I would be ok. This was indeed the case, we finished 8th, so that period of consolidation was achieved, but times were changing.

Football & Christmas Don't Mix

I never appreciated how much football and Christmas did not really mix until I became involved at Fulham F.C.

With such a busy schedule of games over the busy Christmas period if you were involved in preparing opposition match reports which needed a very quick turnaround, which I was, it meant that I could not over indulge as I was often called upon to undertake such reports.

I recall one year on Boxing Day I was required to do a match report on Southampton as we were playing them the following week.

Unfortunately, they were not playing locally but at home in

Southampton. The K.O. was 12 noon.

With me living in Lincoln in was effectively a 600+ mile round trip. This meant that Christmas day was a non-event, as I would have to leave home around 5.30am on Boxing Day to make sure I was there in plenty of time. We won the game the following week 1-0 if I am correct, so I had done my job.

The reason I recall this day in particular because, on the way to Southampton (December the 26th 2004) the news broke there had been a been a giant Tsunami which turned out to be the worst catastrophe and loss of life in living memory.

I always spare a thought for the people caught up in the Tsunami every Boxing Day as a result of this tragedy.

The same could be said for New Year, I was often called upon to go to a game on and around this period, which meant depending on the journey, I would be in bed when the clock struck midnight, and in any case not able to over indulge as I would be driving early on New Year's Day.

This was the norm if you were involved in preparing match reports, which I was at both Fulham and Manchester City until the season we won the Premiership title for the first time in the season 2011/12.

For the 2012/13 season for some unknown reason Roberto Mancini decided he did not want match reports any longer from the Scouts, but reports were to be done by analysts and a few people he brought in. To say I was not best pleased is an understatement as these reports accounted for 80% of my work.

The players and staff have to make sacrifices around this period, but so do the Scouts which tends to be overlooked.

Security for Roman Abramovich

I had been sent to Middlesbrough to do a match report on Chelsea, I had been allocated a Director's seat on the away side of the box about five rows from the front on the aisle.

As always, I try to get to my seat early to watch the warm up, you can pick up good information from the warm up, like certain players boot colour, hair style and colour, to left foot or right foot preference - which can be checked when the game kicks off.

I went towards the box entrance and proceeded through towards my seat. There were two well-dressed gentlemen standing on either side of the entry/exit to the box. I showed one of them my ticket, thinking they were stewards of the club, he shrugged his shoulders and said it was nothing to do with him. I had apparently just asked one of Mr Abramovich's security staff the way to my seat. I gestured an apology to the security guard and took my seat.

It's not an overly big Directors' Box and it goes back behind me another 4 or 5 rows.

After about 10 minutes there was a sudden movement by both security staff - Mr Abramovich was entering the box, he came towards me nodded and sat two rows in front of me.

The box was still quite empty when suddenly there was a further commotion behind me, someone had jumped into the Director's Box and was heading for the Chelsea owner. As quick as a flash the security staff became bodyguards.

As one of them got level with me he reached inside his breast pocket, I don't think it was for a pen to get the guys autograph, or even just for a scratch (I'll leave you to speculate).

Apparently, that's exactly what the intruder wanted Roman Abramovich's autograph. It was all over in a flash, as things went back to normal, the body guard who was first to react and put his hand inside his jacket, looked straight at me, nodded and said nothing but gave a wry smile as if to say – 'You saw nothing'.

As I left the stadium Mr Abramovich's cars were parked at the main area, I could see people with some detectors checking under the car for any unknown devices.

The following week I was allocated Chelsea again, this time at Leicester City. As I walked into the Executive Lounge, Mr Abramovich was coming the other way. The security/bodyguard who I had seen the previous week saw me, realising he had seen me the week before but kept a close watch on me, he seemed then to recall my face and went back into observation routine.

When I left the stadium, around 10 minutes before the end, I noticed that Mr Abramovich's cars were parked outside the stadium. The main reception was again being checked over with devices that they were using to check under the car, I can only assume for booby traps or explosives.

I picked up the pace to get back to my car.

Season's between 2005 & 2008

The 2005/06 season began under the new management of Stuart Pearce. We retained our Premiership place but finished 15th, consolidation again, but I had a feeling everything Kevin had said about the lack of investment was starting to put a strain on the club's position to remain there.

The 2006/07 season was our toughest yet. We finished 14th and were fighting a relegation battle for most of the season.

During that season, I had been asked by Stuart to go and see a young talent called Michael Johnson. He was a 17/18-year-old, playing for England under 19s.

Lynda came with me for company, to be honest I wonder sometimes who the scout is, me or her? She can be very harsh and unforgiving on what she thinks of a player, especially highly paid players!

We were less than ten minutes into the game when Lynda said "This boy looks great" I was still assessing him, but she was right. He totally dominated the midfield, he slotted passes into channels that split the defence time and time again.

His touch, control and vision were very impressive. He was the best young talent I had ever seen. The game finished and we drove the long journey back to Lincoln and arrived home in the very early hours, only to be woken up (I remember it well,) at 9.01am.

Stuart Pearce was on the phone, I remember saying to Stuart "You're early," he said he had seen some remarks in the media about Michael's performance the night before and had been waiting almost 2 hours to ring me (after 9.00am).

I started to wax lyrical about Michael, I said "This boy is ready for the first team now."

He was given a very good contract.

Unfortunately, things went wrong. A combination of injuries and the fact he struggled to come to terms with professional football; getting into bad habits off the field meant that he eventually played his final game in 2009, at home to Scunthorpe in the Carling Cup. I was there, he scored a stunning goal from long range, dominated the game, but it was a false dawn. Everybody thought he is on his way back, subsequent managers tried to rehabilitate him but to no avail.

The club stood by him longer than would be the norm in the hope that he would make a comeback. However, on 28th December 2012 the club's patience ran out and he was released. The club had been paying him all this time without making the problems he was having off the field public knowledge, but he was getting into all sorts so in the end Manchester City said enough is enough.

When you consider he was born in 1988, what a player we could have had in our current rise to prominence. It does not bear thinking about, such a talent that was never fulfilled.

There had been rumours of a possible £82m takeover, which eventually went through in June 2007, but not before Stuart had been sacked by the board on the 14th May.

The new owner was a man called Thaksin Shinawatra, who did not turn out to be the saviour everyone thought he was going to be.

Sven-Goran Erickson was appointed manager for the 2007/2008 season.

Things were about to take off, however, I was now going to be tested to see if I would be kept on as I no longer knew the manager, it was wait and see time.

During the 2007/08 season, under Sven and the new ownership, money was found, and the squad was enhanced. We started very well, in the top 5 for nearly 2/3 months of the season, but we tailed off towards the end and we finished 9th. Although, we qualified for Europe again through the fair play system, Sven was sacked on the 2nd of June 2008 with Mark Hughes installed as manager on the 1st July 2008. This was to prove a pivotal change, Mark Hughes brought quite a few staff with him.

7

TAKEOVER & TITLES!

Season - 2008/09

On the morning of the 1st September, the club changed forever with a £200m take-over on the last day of the transfer window, which showed immediately the intentions of the new owners Sheikh Mansour and the new chairman Khaldoon al Mubarak.

There were concerns that this was going to be a plaything, a real-life Subbuteo thing, just a new toy. With this being the last day of the transfer window, no one expected what was going to happen next.

Three minutes before the end of the window we made our first signing Robinho, from Real Madrid for a UK record fee of £32.5m. If there were any doubts about the intentions of the new owners, then this was sending out a clear message.

We meant business!

Little did we know what was going to happen; it was light the blue touch paper and see the rocket take off and pick up speed, season after season.

Mark Hughes brought in his own team for scouting and recruitment. This was the first time I really felt under threat, he brought in Mike Rigg to oversee everything, he appointed some 'elite' scouts, as they were called, on a full-time basis. Men such as, Rob Newman ex-professional with Norwich - he had played for them in Europe. John Gannon had played for the Crazy Gang at Wimbledon among others. Barry Hunter ex-professional, Alan Watson (who became my immediate boss) and Gary Worthington among others.

This was crunch time for me, I was no longer known to the people making the decisions. We were summoned to a meeting and I was offered a part time contract on a salary much higher than I had been on + expenses. But this meant a greater commitment. I accepted, provided I could handle the extra workload.

I soon made my mark and felt, despite the experienced 'elite' scouts, I was holding my own still involved heavily with match reports (which the 'elite' scouts have never done) working closely with two guys, Dave Fallows and Pedro Marques, who had been brought in from Portugal to oversee the match opponent reports.

I was feeling more secure again, as the feedback from Mark Hughes and his staff was very positive.

Pictures of: Rob Newman, left, Neil Richardson & John Gannon, right.

The Faroe Islands Trip

As we were now in European competitions European match reports were required. We had been drawn to play and I went with Graham Carr to make the report; I did the report while Graham did the PR etc.

But as we were about to land, I realised that Graham, although a seasoned traveller did not like flying. We were approaching the Faroe Islands and had started our descent, we had to fly in between two mountains which by now were higher than the plane, I could see Graham getting a grip on the arm of the seat and heard him say "F****** hell I don't like that."

Anyway, we landed, Graham was fine and no more was said. An agent called Jacob met us in a 4x4 and was going to take us to the capital Torshavn and to the hotel.

He said, "I will take you the scenic route", so we set off and started to climb getting higher and higher on a very narrow road, now with a sheer drop on one side off hundreds of meters.

I was in the back and Graham was in front of me, Jacob driving from the left (the sheer drop side). As we got higher and higher the mist and clouds were now all around us. The scenic route was not so scenic at all, we couldn't see a thing. Jacob's phone rang which he answered - hands free - I think, he then proceeded to send a text using another phone. I could see Graham getting a little agitated the higher we climbed and the clouds were getting thicker. By now Jacob was driving with his hands off the steering wheel using his knees whilst texting and speaking on the phone.

Graham could hold himself no longer he said in a firm voice.

"F****** hell Jacob, if we go off the road here it won't be a ******* seat belt we'll need, it will be a ******* parachute!"

Jacob could see Graham was not happy (neither was I to be truthful, but I kept quiet), Jacob stopped what he was doing and started driving normally. We have laughed about it ever since.

The stadium, if you can call it that, was the most picturesque ground I have ever had the privilege to scout at. You can imagine the Norwegian fjords; the pitch was carved out of the side of the mountain. My seat was a long plank four or five rows deep. I was on the fifth highest. To my left was a large mountain which fell away down to the sea and an inlet. Behind one of the goals was a small club house, where we were entertained. On the opposite side of the pitch was the edge of the mountain with a large net running alongside the pitch, to catch any balls to stop them falling down the mountain side.

The dangerous bit was that our seats were six feet or so from the main road behind us, you could see and hear the traffic as it passed behind.

On a nice, sunny, warm day, it was difficult to concentrate on the game and not the scenery.

The day we were leaving the island, Graham said he wanted me to come back next week and do a follow up report seeing as I now knew a bit more about the place.

I said fine and asked if he was coming back as well.

Graham replied, "Not f***ing likely, it's far too f***ing dangerous trying to land, never mind that, we haven't taken off yet, not to mention the seat two yards from the road with no barriers, you're on your own."

So, I was coming back next weekend, I told my son who said, "Strange Dad, but I have always wanted to go to the Faroe Islands."

I arranged a flight and he could stay in my room; I covered the cost of items like breakfast etc, above what Manchester City were due to pay (I never have found out why he wanted to go to the Faroe Islands).

Everything was going well; we went for a meal and a drink in the town. Wherever we went, people seemed to know who we were and gave us a great welcome, word seemed to get around, as we went from bar to bar, they were expecting us!

The game was the next day, so I did not want to stay out late with the kick-off around 1pm. Paul said, "I think I will stay out for a while Dad."

I told him not to be too late, it was about 10pm when I headed back out of town to my hotel and left Paul heading for a bar. I was tired and went straight to bed. I woke up about 1am - nb sign of Paul, I tried ringing him but there was no answer. I tried again about 1.45am - still no answer, by now I was getting anxious and could not get back to sleep.

This continued most of the night and I was now worried, I got dressed and went to go and look for him around 6am. I had not slept a wink; he was in a strange country never mind a strange place and he was not answering his phone. My mind was working overtime, I even asked the hotel to check with the local police to see if there had been any trouble in the town, he checked and said all had been quiet. That helped, but there was still no sign of Paul.

It was now around 6.15am, I was knackered and had a game to report on in a few hours and my son was missing; unable to contact him via his phone.

As I left the hotel to go and find him, he came strolling around the corner, big smile on his face.

"What you are doing up at this time?" he asked.

With a mixture of relief and anger, I gave him a hug, then tore into him.

"What am I doing? - you f****** arse, I've been trying to find you! That's why I have not slept a wink and you didn't answer your phone."

"Oh sorry," he said, "never heard it."

"You never heard it where the f*** were you I have been worried sick!" I ranted.

"People seemed to know who we were, and they kept buying me drinks, then I got invited to a house party, people have been so nice Dad" he calmly replied.

That nearly started me off again, but I was just happy that he was safe and sound. Panic over, it was time to get some sleep, as I had a game to watch in a few hours. I went to the loo and was talking to Paul from the bathroom saying about what time we were getting picked up. As I came out of the bathroom, he was in bed fast asleep. The little s*** was now even asleep before me, but I took great pleasure in waking him up when my alarm went off.

He was as right as rain when we got to the ground as if he had had a good night's sleep, I was knackered.

I did the report which did not change much from the first report, we won both legs and went onto the next round.

It was a Saturday, there were no flights on a Sunday, so we stayed till the Monday. Most places were closed, apparently, the locals only go out on a Friday because it is too expensive with a pint around £7 - £8.

We had a quiet night in the hotel before flying home on the Monday. Paul thanked me and apologised for keeping me awake, we laugh about it now, he really enjoyed his trip to the Faroe Islands. I forgave him, but he never went on another scouting trip with me!

I was to become heavily involved in travelling to Europe, which on reflection, may well have been the club testing me to see if I was up to the challenge.

This was a new and exciting experience, I was later to go on and do reports on our group stage opponents Twente Enschede (Netherlands), PSG (France), Racing Santander (Spain) and Schalke (Germany).

We won the group and progressed to the knockout stages before finally losing in the quarter finals to Hamburg. I did no more games after the group stage but had done enough to be regarded as a member of the scouting and recruitment department.

Danger in Venezuela

I was asked to go to Venezuela to watch the South American under 20's tournament, involving the best International teams, including Brazil, Argentina, Uruguay, etc.

It was a long flight and I only had an economy class seat, I found out later that Jim Lawlor, from M********* United, was in business class.

When we arrived in Caracas, we had been advised to gather at a given meeting point and not to, under any circumstances, wander off from the main area on our own.

As we were all gathered having a roll call, I heard some very senior names in football being called out, working for some very well-respected clubs like Milan, Juventus, Barcelona, PSG, Chelsea and M********* United to name a few.

The chief scout at M********* United had a broad Irish accent, we introduced ourselves.

We were huddled together and told to follow the armed security arranged for us, which was a little disconcerting, onto a waiting bus. We were advised that Caracas was the murder capital of the world and people have been known to wander off and get kidnapped and a ransom note demanded. That made me really comfortable - not!

We proceeded as requested and we all kept very close, being the least experienced of the people representing their respective clubs, I kept very close to Jim from Man Utd he was a tall, 6ft plus guy.

I was in exalted company, and on this trip was way out of my depth to be honest. Some big names, some big clubs were present, this would have been around 2009. I decided very quickly that I had to get myself in order and get organised for the two-week competition.

We were all taken to the coach by the security arranged by the company, to keep us safe whilst in Venezuela.

When we got on the coach some 20 or so other scouts from all over the world were there. We all had our names and clubs checked. When the roll call was finished, we were told the following journey to the hotel will be approximately 45 minutes. We were also advised that there would be an armed guard with us all the way both in front and behind us. We were further advised that in the event of a kidnap attempt, to get on the ground and stay there.

I was feeling nervous before, but now I was positively on tenterhooks.

At this point, just as we were about to set off for the hotel, Jim Lawlor piped up and in his broad Irish accent said loudly, so that everyone could hear.

"Well, if we are attacked get everybody on the bus to point at John from Manchester City. Tell them to just take him as he is worth more than all of us put together."

Everyone laughed. It released the tension a little and Jim and I have become great friends on the scouting circuit, we always share a laugh when we meet.

Jim has a great sense of humour. He once told me Sir Alex wanted to sign a 'big name' striker. Jim suggested 'Jan Vennegoor of Hesselink' - that's a big name. I said to him that a few years ago we could not even sign a player called 'Jo'.

When we got back to Manchester, we shared a taxi from the airport, and he dropped me off at our training ground. "For God's sake don't mention to Sir Alex if you see him that MUFC paid the fare", he said, half joking but, I think, half serious.

Another name I would like to mention from the Venezuela trip is a guy called Pete de-Visser from Chelsea, he was in his 70's then. He told a story one night about how he got taken on at Chelsea. Pete was from Holland and football obsessed, he never stopped talking about football he is, I understand, a legend in his own lifetime which I can believe.

When I tell you what he says, try and imagine a broken English accent in Dutch tone it works better.

He explained that Roman Abramovich had heard about him and wanted him to join Chelsea. He asked Pete to join him and others onto his yacht to discuss things.

Roman had his usual advisers around him, as discussions took place Pete explained he kept very quiet; various players were mentioned, and everyone seemed to be agreeing with whatever Roman had mentioned.

Pete told us how he eventually had had enough and said,

"Some people in this room are talking s*** and telling you what you want to hear, not what is right, and if you want me to join Chelsea get them out of this room and we shall speak, you have already wasted over £150 million on below average players that these people have recommended."

I will tell you the truth, not what you want to hear. Mr Abramovich told all to leave except Pete. He was appointed to the staff and the rest is history.

On another night he noticed that I was limping I usually wore shorts, but I had been badly bitten, I can only assume by mosquitoes and my legs were a mess.

Pete asked me to show him. Reluctantly I obliged, but I needed persuading. I rolled my tracksuit bottoms up.

"That's not good," Pete said, "Do you have anything to take?" I didn't.

"I have a magic stick which you roll onto each bite and it kills the infection at source." I told him thanks, but I'd be fine, I did not wish to bother him.

"No! you need my stick," I still resisted his offer until he said, "I was in Africa a few years ago and a friend of mine was badly bitten just like you. I offered him the magic stick he, like you, refused."

"And?" I asked.

"And he was dead in the morning" Pete replied.

"Where is the stick and can I keep it." I also got treatment from the Brazil team doctor. Pete and I got on very well after that and is a legend in my mind.

I spent two weeks in South America in total, watching over 200 players in that time; a completely different experience to what I was used to. I came back with a couple of recommendations but nothing materialised.

My first pick was Douglas Costa playing for Brazil; his club side was Gremio in Brazil, but we never bought him. He did sign for Shakhtar Donetsk for £6m soon afterwards and has played for the senior Brazilian team on a regular basis. Currently he is playing for Juventus in Italy, (2019).

My other main recommendation, which again we did not sign, was a midfield player called Sandro who signed for Spurs for £6m. I mentioned before about being frustrated. I'd spent two weeks in South America, came back with two recommendations and nothing came from it. That is the norm and you must get used to it because often there is a bigger picture. But again, a great learning experience.

On the bright side, other than having a great learning experience, I was asked to go full time after I returned from the tournament.

In terms of City, we finished 10th in the League, which was deemed not good enough and were knocked out early in both domestic cup competitions.

Ukraine & the Black Limo

During the close season in England, I was sent to the Ukraine to watch the under 21s and the full International squad. The following day, I was met by an agent, who took me to my hotel; shortly before going to watch the under 21's. I was aware that people were looking at me, as word had got out that Manchester City were there. I was approached by a young lady who said "at the end of the game could we speak to you?" And I agreed.

At the end of the game she came looking for me and escorted me down to the edge of the pitch, near some boards that you see when players are being interviewed for television.

To my horror, from around the corner came a guy with a TV camera perched on his shoulder and an interpreter. The young lady started speaking to me, which was translated, as well as my response back to her. Apparently, I was live on Ukrainian television, I managed to say things without saying anything, if you know what I mean. I finished the interview unscathed. This was another part of the learning curve negotiated!

I returned to the hotel and all was going well. When I got up the next morning, there was a note. I was given the following instructions:

"Could I get a taxi or walk to the stadium (which was not far away). Outside the ground you will see a car with the number plate xxx xxx, they will have your ticket".

I went to the stadium looking for the car as described. I spotted the number plate; it was on a big black limo with blacked out windows. As I got there, I knocked on the rear window. It came down about halfway; a hand appeared holding a ticket. I took the ticket and the window closed. Nothing had been said, I just walked away and entered the stadium. No idea what it was all about.

I met up with the agent, but I decided to keep quiet and say nothing. That night he took me to a restaurant we had a nice local meal.

At this point he started fishing to see if I was impressed with any of his players, I had become quite adept at avoiding difficult questions. He then suggested we go to a local club where there were plenty of young, pretty, Ukrainian girls that he could introduce me to. I apologised made my excuses and headed back to the hotel.

The Serbian Connection

Many clubs get contacted by agents trying to push their players, so a good relationship with them can pay dividends, but conversely you must be careful as a club, to keep a balanced approach. One thing that clubs do is use their contacts and agents abroad, which is a God send, when people like me go abroad. The agent we have a relationship with, will look after the visiting scout.

In some places you would not go on your own, in others it's not a problem, the agent will do the basic things like arrange transport to the stadium, usually they will collect you from the airport and ferry you around. Making sure you are well looked after; many also take you out for meals etc. For places like Ukraine, Serbia, South America, often countries where English is not spoken widely, it is a must in my opinion.

We had been contacted about a young player playing for Vojvodina a team in the topflight in Serbia. He was apparently 16 years of age (no names I am afraid). We had been advised that he had made his senior international debut recently at this tender age and was being touted around the big clubs, and we should see him before he gets snapped up.

I was sent to Belgrade on a Saturday morning on a very early flight, to take a game in on the Saturday in Belgrade, then on Sunday I'd be driven an hour away to take in Vojvodina v Partizan Belgrade. Without an agent or in this case two, it would have been very difficult to achieve this on your own.

I checked into the hotel, the club arranged for flights, hotels etc, on this occasion the agents were looking after the tickets, transport and as it turned out all the meals. There was nothing of any real interest in the Saturday game, but the real reason I was there was for the young lad on the Sunday.

After the game on Saturday the agents took me to a very nice restaurant in Belgrade. We had been there about 20 minutes or so when there seemed to be a commotion near where we were sitting. A man appeared, surrounded by an entourage of what looked like bodyguards. He was heading our way; I must have looked bemused and concerned because one of the agents told me everything was all right.

He kept coming straight towards our table, he stopped and said, "I understand you are from Manchester", I said nervously that I was, he went onto say that if I needed anything, to please contact him and that he hoped I enjoyed my stay. At this point he handed me a business card. Fortunately, I also had my business cards on me, so I passed one to him. I still had not read his, as he turned to walk away with people all around making a fuss of him.

At this point I looked at his card, I still have it attached to the fridge next to a magnet of the Serbian flag.

HRH Crown Prince Alexander

Royal Palace 11040 Belgrade Serbia

I was taken aback to say the least.

I never found out how he knew who I was or how he knew I would be in that restaurant, unless the agents had tipped him off and were trying to make an impression to influence me!

Arrangements were made to pick me up the next day to travel to Vojvodina to watch the 16-year-old supposed to be superstar with a full International cap to his name.

Just as I was leaving the car one of the agents told me we would be having lunch at a five-star hotel near the ground and we had to go, we cannot turn it down. When I asked why not, I was just told that we can't refuse, and that it would all be explained the next day. I was intrigued but had no idea what was going on, but I could do nothing about it.

The next morning, I was picked up early as the drive was over an hour and we had a mysterious lunch engagement that I still knew nothing about. As we were nearing the hotel for lunch I was enlightened as to why it had been a secret until now.

We had been summoned to have lunch with the owner, Chairman etc. of Vojvodina at his hotel. I thought the reason I was kept in the dark was, so I had no time to think about the job in hand. I could not have been further from the truth to a certain extent, though I feel there was a hidden agenda.

The agents went on to tell me we were having lunch with someone called Bata Kan Kan.

I was then told that he was allegedly head of the Serbian mafia and was suspected of involvement in numerous murders. He had recently also survived attempts on his own life.

The best way to describe him is that he had a look of eccentricity about him, in the way he dressed, with big gold medallions around his neck and with bright clothes to match.

I remember thinking at the time if he wanted to stay low and incognito, to make it hard for would-be assassins - then he was not doing a very good job!

The table was oval and seated about eight people. The first thing I noticed was that he was sitting with a brick wall about two feet from his back, a bodyguard sat to his immediate right, then me with my back to a full glass window facing onto the lounge area. The agents were sat on the other side of the table with their backs towards the massive gardens, others slotted into the spare seats.

He did not speak English, so everything was translated through his bodyguard, a young menacing looking guy with long hair tied back into a ponytail down past his shoulders.

As we sat down some eight or so actual bodyguards surrounded us all facing away from the table

Watching for anything out of the norm. To say it was disconcerting is not the phrase I am looking for......more like I was s******* myself.

The guy to my left thought he was helping when he said, "Don't worry these bodyguards are well trained to spot danger."

Well that made me feel much better – not!

I could not wait to get out of there, but there was nothing I could do.

General conversation took place through the interpreter. His bodyguard asked if I had a family, I said I did, a wife called Lynda, and a son, Paul who works in the gambling trade with William Hill.

Straight away he asked me point blank, did I want to know the results of games in two weeks' time. I politely declined his offer.

I found out afterwards that he controlled matters in Belgrade, such as organised trouble as part of the ultra-type of 'supporter', they liaise with opposition so-called 'supporters' to organise the violence.

He assured me that because of my presence at today's game, which he said would have had trouble as both teams 'supporters' hate each other, that there would be no trouble they did not want to look bad.

Bata Kan Kan continued to speak through his interpreter. He told us he had spoken to the team manager and the boy would start, so I was now influencing the team selection as well as crowd behaviour!

All seemed to be well with no problems as we set off for the game. There was no sign of trouble, so he was as good as his word in that respect.

As we were leaving, Bata Kan Kan said that the next time I visited, I must stay in his hotel, he said he would arrange some entertainment for me, no doubt to sweeten my report.

I understood later that he meant he would leave a selection of ladies in my room for me. I leave it to your imagination what he meant by the offer.

The team sheet arrived, and the boy was not starting, he was only on the bench. Bata was not impressed, he was fuming, not only had he given me his word the boy was playing, the agent said that he felt stupid as a result. The manager had also made it look as if he did not control his people, no doubt in a much wider sense than just football.

The next thing I noticed was that he was sat directly in front of me, bright colours medallions and all in all, the perfect target for anyone wanting to take a pop at him from distance. The problem was I was sat within a couple of feet, just behind him.

If there was going to be another attempt on his life, he was making it easy to pick him out in a crowd, what I was worried about was a sniper missing him and hitting me.

If you Google Bata Kan Kan, you will see why I was concerned.

At half-time he disappeared, and I saw him walking across the running track that surrounded the pitch, towards the dressing rooms. He re-appeared as the players returned to the field with his arm around the young 16-year-old, obviously telling him I was here to watch him.

The boy was no better than average, a few nice touches but nothing special, to be honest if he knew what was occurring it would not have helped his nerves, so basically, although it was only 45 minutes I could report upon, but it was not going to be positive, as some of the basics were missing.

I felt on the way back to the hotel that the agents knew it as well, but I told them I will send in my report as usual, and someone will be in touch.

I went to bed wondering how he had been given a full International cap at the tender age of 16 as he did not look anything special. I later found out that someone had allegedly paid the Serbian FA to give him a cap to boost his transfer fee. How true that was no one knows!

Following that eventful trip, I followed the young boy's progress, he was watched by others and we all came to the same conclusion - not for us!

I understand that on the Tuesday after the match the manager was sacked for making Bata Kan Kan look a fool!

About 18 months after I had been to lunch with Bata Kan Kan, and following unsuccessful attempts on his life, he was found dead, I believe in unexplained circumstances, in his bath in the very hotel he offered to put me up in. Say no more!

Season - 2009/10

Mark Hughes was starting the new season under pressure and he was controversially sacked on the 19th December 2009, following seven consecutive draws in the Premiership.

He was replaced by Roberto Mancini on 20th December 2009 and things were really going to take off.

With a sudden change in management, Mark Hughes being sacked just prior to Christmas, my future was, once again, thrown into the air. My only saving grace was that most of the staff there in the department did not change.

I had survived at Fulham with Jean Tigana and at City with Sven and Mark. So, I was feeling more confident that I was going to be retained on my ability alone. I had gone through a very steep learning curve up until now but over the next few years, it was going to be even steeper.

I was being used more and more, not only for match reports but player recruitment, I was now being asked to go abroad more and more often, both for players and European match reports.

Now that I was on a full-time contract, I received more privileged feedback, which added to the frustration.

We finished fifth in the Premiership this season.

Season - 2010/11

Things would never be the same again, looking back, these were the times when everything I'd learned over the previous years would help me more and more the more I got involved; from what had started in 1998 as a hobby, I was now in a full-time role, in the thick of things playing a major role in match report assessment and player recruitment.

I was now traveling abroad much more, including match reports on our Champions League opponents. I recall watching Lech Poznan in Poland, coming back and saying when they score the whole crowd turn their back on the pitch link arms and jump up and down, it provides for a great atmosphere.

We, as a team, adopted that celebration and still do it from time to time, I remember at the 2011 FA Cup final against Stoke City, when we scored everyone in the Manchester City seats stood up and did what was to become known as "The Poznan".

About that final, the scouts and their wives were taken to London for two nights, tickets for the cup final - all expenses paid. It had taken a little while, but success was about to become the norm.

I also recall that prior to the Cup Final, I was sent to Blackpool to watch Stoke and do a report; it was their penultimate match before the Final. I still have a copy of my report which was the final document used by Roberto Mancini in the match preparations, that put added pressure on when watching the game. The pictures you see are not the whole report.

To sum up what you see in these pictures, they were a defensively disciplined side that relied on their Target Man, Kenwyne Jones, to either hold play up bringing other players into the game or crafting out a chance for a shot on goal himself. (See In Possession diagram page 134.)

Stoke's greatest threat was their set pieces. Mainly their throw ins as they were a team who effectively had a specialist throw in taker, Rory Delap, he was a capable footballer and had a lethal long-range throw which we had to be aware of. As you can see from the image, he would throw it into the six-yard box towards Ryan Shawcross. As the ball was thrown in, Huth, Jones & Walters would attack the six-yard box; should the opposition head the ball away, they had Pennant and Whitehead on the edge of the area to strike from range. (See Long Throws diagram page 135.)

When defending set pieces, they are very cautious. Almost everyone

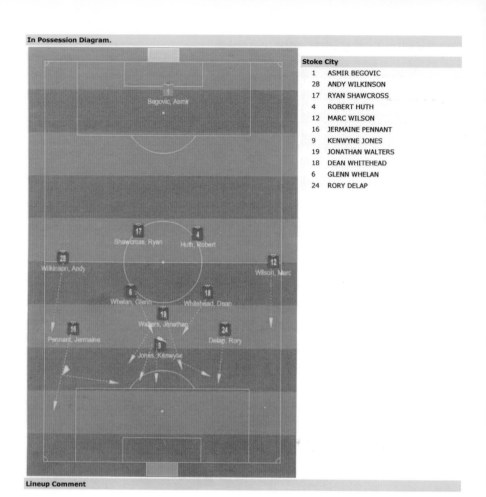

Stoke City	
1	ASMIR BEGOVIC
28	ANDY WILKINSON
17	RYAN SHAWCROSS
4	ROBERT HUTH
12	MARC WILSON
16	JERMAINE PENNANT
9	KENWYNE JONES
19	JONATHAN WALTERS
18	DEAN WHITEHEAD
6	GLENN WHELAN
24	RORY DELAP

Lineup Comment

is brought back to defend apart from Jermaine Pennant, who they try and use as an outlet for breakaways. That was a danger because he was pacey, and their defenders were strong and excellent aerially. (See Defensive Corner diagram page 136.)

My advice to exploit them was to keep the ball on the ground and play it out wide at tempo to drag the full backs out of possession allowing a runner to exploit this space. This will then force the centre backs out wide to try and cover for that mistake potentially leading to a chance.

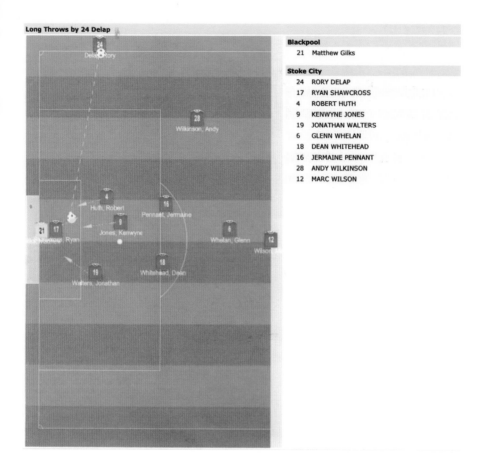

Blackpool

21	Matthew Gilks

Stoke City

24	RORY DELAP
17	RYAN SHAWCROSS
4	ROBERT HUTH
9	KENWYNE JONES
19	JONATHAN WALTERS
6	GLENN WHELAN
18	DEAN WHITEHEAD
16	JERMAINE PENNANT
28	ANDY WILKINSON
12	MARC WILSON

I kicked every ball, headed every ball away, made tackles shouted instructions from the second tier of Wembley (although no one could have heard me) but it made me feel better and relieved the tension.

We had made that crucial breakthrough winning a trophy for the first time in many years, the rocket was starting to pick up pace. We were in for an exciting ride, things were happening both on and off the field at a rapid pace, money was available to move to the next level, plans were in place to build a brand-new training ground and develop an academy, both of which are now finished and state of the art.

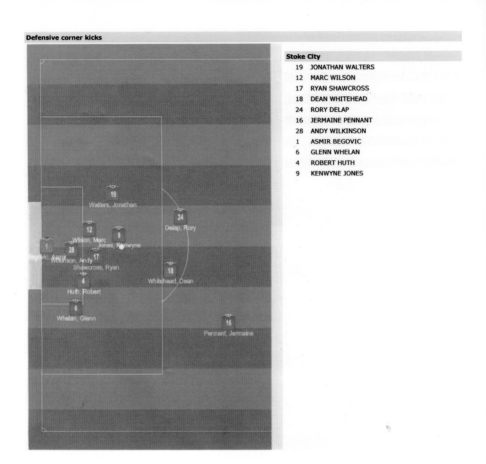

Stoke City

19	JONATHAN WALTERS
12	MARC WILSON
17	RYAN SHAWCROSS
18	DEAN WHITEHEAD
24	RORY DELAP
16	JERMAINE PENNANT
28	ANDY WILKINSON
1	ASMIR BEGOVIC
6	GLENN WHELAN
4	ROBERT HUTH
9	KENWYNE JONES

I am always impressed with the facilities when I go to the campus. I was there recently for a four-day global scouts conference, with scouts coming from all over the world. I was put up in one of the bedrooms we have for the first team to use (sole occupancy) prior to games. I stayed in the first team quarter, room 25 which I understand to be Fernandinho's room and his squad number.

The whole complex is unique and has all the teams under one roof including the ladies' team, who are also successful.

I was told when I was there that we are taking boys into the system from age six. Can you believe it? Glad I didn't get involved until they are 17 or thereabouts!

We finished that season 3rd in the league on goal difference.

Season - 2011/12

This was to be a season I will never experience again - I am sure of that.

We were on a roll and started with confidence I was still heavily involved on a full-time basis, covering match reports as usual, as well as other duties.

We were never out of the first two from the start, we were now buying players like Balotelli (love him or hate him) he had a crucial part to play especially on the final day. We had Joe Hart, I had been to see him play for Shrewsbury Town at Boston United and given him an "A" - remember the marking code - sign him!

Well we did for £600,000.

There was Sergio Aguero, what a part he had to play, David Silva and not forgetting Vincent Kompany amongst so many others I could name.

There were some crucial games, but the most memorable early game was away at M********* United on the 23rd of October.

We were doing something special, winning the game 1-6 at Old Trafford. No one could believe it; we had sent out a signal of intent away at Old Trafford. Nobody does that to them on their own patch, the rocket was well and truly on its way and would get faster and faster.

A story was doing the rounds the morning after the 1-6 drubbing that Sir Alex got home that evening and had his customary drink of wine, in fact he had a little more than usual, which in the circumstances was not surprising. He went to bed with his wife and fell into a good sleep only to feel a dig in his ribs in the morning.

"Alex, Alex its 7." His wife was shouting.

Sir Alex replied, "F***! They've not scored again have they?!"

Sorry, Sir Alex, I have met him a few times and he seemed nice, I am sure he would not mind, as he has taken the piss out of Manchester City for over two decades. Just the Mancunian sense of humour. Little did we know that come the end of the season with a 10 goal turn around how important that result was going to be.

As the season progressed, we were very consistent, never out of the first two. It was a two-horse race in the end with Arsenal finishing around 19 points behind us and United who both finished on 89 points.

We were scheduled to play United on the 30th April 2012 with everybody saying it was winner takes all. Whoever won that game would win the league especially United.

As the last three fixtures drew closer and closer whoever was doing the match reports had a big job on their hands but usually the games were spread out so as to get varied opinions. The first game that needed covering was United away at Wigan. I got the call, could I do a report on United, the second fixture was on United at home to Aston Villa.

I thought well I got the first game, so I wouldn't get the second as well. Wrong! I got the call again to watch United against Aston Villa at Old Trafford. At that game I bumped into David Moyes. He knew my face having seen him around the circuit, but he did not know my name. I introduced myself and told him who I was with.

"We could do with you doing us a favour next week." I told him.

"I will do my best." He replied.

Well having done the first and second, last game pressure was off and onto whoever got the final game before we played them on the 30th April 2012. The game was to be on the 22nd at home to Everton. Well to my surprise I got the call again, to do the final report, I could not believe it, but as far as confidence was concerned mine was sky high. Everton had sent David Moyes the previous week to watch United, Manchester City had sent me to watch the last three. I was buzzing.

As a side note my wife Lynda and two of our friends Joy and Eileen hatched a plan for me to take them shopping or drop them off at the Trafford Centre and pick them up afterwards. I was now an unpaid chauffeur with the most important game I had ever reported awaiting me.

When you do three back-to-back reports it can become both repetitious and predictable to a certain extent. I had spotted a few things that needed pointing out but one tactic United used, which stood out above all others was how they used Paul Scholes at attacking set pieces.

They would get set as usual and Scholes would stand in and around the 'D' in a central area. As the corner kick was taken, he would drop back 2 or 3 yards ready to pick up the knock back or knock down, effectively the second ball and get a shot away. He had done this nearly 12 times over the three games, so this was a pre-planned training ground move.

He had made the keeper make saves five or six times but could easily have resulted in goals.

I watched the game and left with 10 minutes to go to avoid the rush and headed for the Trafford Centre with United winning 4-2. On the way home from games I always try and replay some of the things to get them clear in my head. No chance with Joy, Eileen, and Lynda talking all the way home! Just before I got to the Trafford Centre, I turned the radio on to hear to my surprise and amazement Everton had scored twice in the last seven minutes to snatch a draw. We were now in the driving seat, provided we beat United at home. David Moyes and Everton had done us that favour after all.

The pressure was full on now with the reports.

What normally happens is the game is put onto the Scout 7 system, that I mentioned previously. Much of what I needed to do had already been recorded in the previous reports. I struggled to sleep that night, so got up very early to complete the third and final report on United.

Something was telling me, instinct I suppose, that the tactic from the corners involving Paul Scholes was going to be vital. I started the report as always, following a set pattern, a tried and tested formula I had developed and carried on developing year after year.

Getting the formation, giving each player a short pen picture, then on to the main body of the report, ending up with the diagrams for all set pieces, dragging players onto the pitch from a set template and explaining who did what.

I got to the corners, I drew the diagrams and went on to explain what happens when the kick is taken. I then decided to add something which turned out to be vital information.

"When the corner kick is taken by United and Paul Scholes drops off, we must, send a player to get in front of him and stop him getting a free shot away. We must stop the opportunity to get a shot on target at all costs."

I finished the report; was more than happy and submitted it as usual.

The game against M********* United was the one we needed to win to get the upper hand and get into pole position for the run in.

The scouts and their wives were invited up to Manchester to watch the United game. To say I was nervous was an understatement, once again I was kicking and heading every ball.

As kick off approached I got more and more nervous. Within a few minutes of the kick-off, United got a corner I am now shouting for somebody to pick up Scholes for the second ball. Again, there was no chance anyone could hear me. I was shouting pick up Scholes and kept repeating it.

As the corner was taken David Silva moved in front of Scholes and blocked the second ball, it looked like somebody had listened to what I said but this was repeated for every corner. Scholes never got a second ball and overall, they never had a shot on target. Ironically, we scored from a corner with Vincent Kompany heading home.

We now had the destiny of the title in our own hands, it was up to us.

The Day We Won the Premier League

We were invited to the final game against QPR, we only needed to win as we had an 8-goal advantage over United on the same points 86.

Things started well we went 1-0 up after 39 minutes and went in at half time feeling secure. However, by the 66th minute we were 1-2 down and looked to have lost our way. United were winning, so it looked as if we were going to throw it away in a game that had seemed a formality. There was a huge air of despair in the stadium.

We scored an equalizer on 90+2 minutes, but this was not enough United were still winning, this in fact made everyone feel worse, we are going to draw and still throw it away.

The rest, as they say, is history with Balotelli setting up Sergio Aguero or Aguerooooooooooooooooo, as he became known to score the winner on 90+4 minutes.

The feeling and emotion of the roller coaster ride, being up then down, then up again, winning it in the fashion we did I don't think will ever be repeated. The 1-6 result at Old Trafford gave us a 10-goal turnaround.

The place went wild grown men and women were in tears; tears of joy and you were hugging people you had never met.

The celebrations began, you made friends with people you had never seen before, even if it was only for a few hours.

I remember walking back to the hotel with Lynda and the other scouts, we were in shock. A City fan coming the other way looked dazed and his eyes showing a degree of confusion.

He stopped us,

"Excuse me, but did we actually win that game and win the Premiership?" He said in an uncertain manner.

"Yes, we did!" We replied.

He went off with a smile as wide as you have ever seen - he was now believing.

	GD	Points
City	+64	89
United	+56	89

We had a great night, but from time to time we had to pinch ourselves and ask each other the same question the man in the street had asked us some hours earlier. We were still in shock.

Could things get any better?

The Maldives & Abu Dhabi

Lynda and I had decided that we wanted to take in a break to the Maldives and combine it with a trip to Abu Dhabi, where our owners resided. Part of the reason was that Manchester City had opened a soccer school in Abu Dhabi and I wanted to see how it worked.

The holiday went well and once the Chief Executive of the island knew I was working for Manchester City, (he was an Arsenal fan), we kept getting invites to parties and dinners, we had a whale of a time. We were treated like VIPs, being involved with such a high-profile club had its perks.

We moved on to Abu Dhabi and stayed in the luxury Emirates Towers Hotel. At first, I did not like Abu Dhabi as much as Dubai, but it grew on me.

We arranged to visit the Manchester City school to see at first-hand how it worked. It was not an academy, but a training school which was also self-funding. Believe me, the parents whose children attended the school were very wealthy and could afford to pay for the privilege. In fact, I felt the guys running the school had to be careful, as they told me that parents offer to pay for things, to make sure their child was involved. They were very careful not to get involved in anything they should not.

I was asked to give a short talk to the watching parents and children, I had not prepared anything and did it off the cuff.

The children sat on the floor with the parents watching, I was introduced as a senior scout from Manchester City working closely with the first team, again I was at the centre of things and the sheiks were now falling over themselves to shake my hand and tell me how good their child was and how much they thought of the school.

I gave a short speech just to tell them what Manchester City was all about and that we were proud to have an owner like Sheik Mansour. I then asked if there were any questions, to my relief no one asked anything and I closed the meeting and just chatted with people individually. Everyone seemed happy, they were very impressed that Manchester City had sent someone to visit them, of course they did not know it was nothing to do with Manchester City, it was off my own back, as I was in Abu Dhabi on holiday.

We left the complex and one of the guys took us back to the hotel where we were staying, feeling once more like royalty, being treated so well by everyone because of my association with Manchester City.

We went on to enjoy the rest of our holiday. It always helped to drop in the conversation that I worked for Manchester City, especially knowing who owned the club, little did they know I had never met the man or was indeed ever likely to, but I let their imaginations take them to where ever they wanted to go.

Towards the end of the holiday, Lynda and I decided to visit Ferrari World where the Abu Dhabi F1 Grand Prix is held, along with a theme park. We were going to go on spec the next day, which was three or four days before the end of our holiday.

We decided to pay a visit to the hotel's cocktail bar on one of the higher floors overlooking the city. We went in the afternoon as it was Happy Hour and therefore more affordable – it's not cheap to drink alcohol in the Emirates. We went up to the bar and surprise, surprise it was empty, we were the only two people in the bar. We decided to just have one and then go, we were a bit embarrassed to be honest.

After about 15 minutes, two men walked into the cocktail bar. The best way I can describe them is that they looked like throwbacks to the gold prospectors in California in the 1800's - especially the one who had a rather grand handlebar moustache.

As we were the only people in the bar they nodded and said hello, I started the conversation by commenting on the stunning view of the city and the ocean.

I seem to remember they were called Buddy and Chuck, when they replied they were obviously from the USA. The small talk began, and they told me they were from Dallas in, Texas. One of them asked where we were from, I thought there was no point in confusing them by saying Lincoln, so I said Manchester. He smiled and asked what we were doing there, and I told him we were just holidaying. When he asked what I did for a living, I told him I was a senior scout for Manchester City FC. What happened next you could not make up. The one with the large moustache shouted to his friend

"You're not going to believe this, these guys come from Manchester and he works for Manchester City."

Well the look on their faces was amazing, "You work for Manchester City the football club?" he said again.

I was surprised they knew who we were especially as they were from the USA, and football was not anywhere as popular as it is now with the MLS.

"Yes, why? - do you know about them? - the owner comes from here Sheikh Mansour." I responded.

"Yes, we know him, we are two of his private pilots, that ferry him and his family around."

To say that knocked us off our feet is an understatement. We started talking, I explained what I did at City and they said they would tell him they had met me.

One of the guys asked when we were going home and I told him it was in a few days, I also told him we were are going to Ferrari World the next day as we had been told it was worth a visit to the home of the Grand Prix.

One of them replied that was a shame, they were busy for the next few days on-call or they would have taken us for a ride in one of Sheikh Mansour's helicopters, to say we were gutted, well what do you think!

We continued to chat and after about 20 minutes, one of the guys asked us if we were definitely going to Ferrari World the next day. I said that we definitely were.

Ten minutes later, one of them returned and said we were all sorted for tomorrow and we had private VIP passes to Ferrari World waiting for us. They will look after you, enable you to jump the queue, if necessary, there was no charge and have a great day. It turned out the cost was over £100, if we had paid, but it cost us nothing.

We went and had a great day riding on the world's fastest roller coaster which was an experience in itself.

Once again being involved with Manchester City had its perks, we were treated like VIPs just because of my association. It's who you know, not what you know, strikes again!

Season - 2012/13

We started the next campaign by winning the Community Shield 3-2, against Chelsea.

I expected the status quo to remain. I had been full time for a few years now and whilst you can never be complacent in football, I was feeling good about the new season under Roberto Mancini. However, the season was nearly under way, I had taken time to recharge the batteries and like all others I was ready to go.

What I did not know as the season was approaching, having been doing opposition match assessments since the start way back in 1998 with Fulham, Roberto Mancini in his wisdom decided he no longer wanted these to be done by the three main scouts, myself, John Graveling and Rod Cousins.

He had brought in his own team from Italy, Aldo Pecini whose name I recognised from my trip to South America (Venezuela) in 2009. Little did I know he would effectively replace me on the match reports.

I understand Aldo, who was a nice guy and I got on well with him in South America and on a subsequent visit to a 7-day tournament in Italy a few years ago, where I recall he said he would tell Roberto what a good scout I was.

Aldo had been the scout that had discovered Roberto and gave him his break, things were starting to fall into place, he was obviously on much more money than me, but as I have said many times, it's who you know, not what you know. Having benefitted from that some years earlier it was now working against me!

The other threat to reporting was coming from a new breed of young analysts who were coming more and more to the fore and could be seen at matches with laptops, filming or taking photos of set pieces. Some clubs banned the use of such equipment. With the technology available now for all kinds of reports, I predict the demise of the old-style scout. Everything you possibly need can be obtained from one scouting tool or another, even to the point of watching a game on a screen in an office that reflects the whole pitch. No need to be at the ground to do your job.

The season had started, and I was still oblivious of the developments. No one had told me anything. I just got on with going where I was being sent but thinking something was not right, I had been doing match reports for 20 years, now nothing was happening.

Then suddenly it all became clear and there was going to be a scouting and recruitment restructure. People were going to lose their jobs due to the onset of new office-based analysts, new and improving technology, you only need watch Sky to see the information that is readily available, it's mind boggling.

Discussions took place with Alan Watson, Gavin Fleig and Gary Worthington.

Rod Cousins, Alex Owen, Peter Morris, Ralph Wright were all leaving the club. That left just myself and John Graveling; John was on a lesser contract than me, but in truth deserved more. I was still on a full-time contract but 80% of my job had gone, so I knew it would not last. For the first time since I started, I felt this might be it with Manchester City, but I had no intention of going elsewhere.

Discussions took place, John G agreed terms, he was going to be paid more than he had been, so it was a no brainer for him. I on the other hand was going to have my salary cut in half. Discussions took place over a short period. I turned the new contract down on 3 or 4 occasions before Gary Worthington and I had one final chat.

Negotiations began; I set out my stall. If I was now going to be on half the money, I wanted a condition that if I went abroad, I would get an extra payment each time I did so. That wasn't the only one I wanted, but I'll spare you the details as I ran out of conditions in the end. Gary made it clear he wanted me to continue and valued my contribution, so I was appointed Senior Scout for the North Region with John G covering the South.

Initially, I have to say I resented the fact that despite being involved heavily in the first Premiership title, I was no longer involved in that area and at the beginning, I missed it. Not now I can assure you though, with the rapid advance of technology. I have seen the reports and whilst they can be described as like my reports, they are more easily put together by the analysts. It used to take me over four hours to do one report whereas, one player report may only take two or three minutes to put onto Scout7. Finally, I was getting my Sunday mornings back after 20 years.

Next time you are watching a game live at a substitution, don't concentrate on the players in question, look at the coach or analyst reading from a manual giving the player going on his instructions, it's probably from the final Scout7 or other system document.

Over the coming months, I would learn that the developments were right, in the way reports were collated but, I still feel that traditional scouting reports could still be incorporated into the new method. It's highly unlikely to happen and with the growing amount of information available about players from many sources, I feel I am a dying breed.

Overall, the season was a disappointment. We finished 2nd in the Premier League & Mancini was sacked two days after the defeat to Wigan in the FA Cup Final. A match at which we were again present

- all expenses paid of course.

Season - 2013/14

Brian Kidd took temporary charge from May 2013 to June 2013, before Manuel Pellegrini became the next permanent manager.

We were about to take things to another level; the rocket which had stalled, began to gradually pick up speed.

We won the Premiership for the second time this time beating West Ham United on the last day and winning the title by 2 points. We also won the League Cup on the 2nd March 2014. Two major trophies, not bad.

We had lost to Wigan in the 6th round of the FA Cup 2-1. We had now lost three times to Wigan in cup competitions, once on my 50th birthday, once in an FA Cup final and now in the 6th round of the FA Cup.

I am not allowed to bet, but if we meet them soon it might be worth a fiver or so. I hope we avoid them in future.

I was at a stage where I was about to re-invent myself now that I was not involved in match reports. The club was growing. We had set up teams in the MLS - New York City, Melbourne City in Australia, Yokohama Marinos, in Japan, Girona in Spain, (who got promoted to the top division in the Spanish La Liga), and one team down in South America, FC Torque.

Now is probably a good time to cover the growth in the club. The club had been expanding at a rapid pace and our scouting meetings were becoming more and more complex. We had meetings in the past with five or six main scouts, now we had people from the USA, Australia, China, South America and all over, not to mention the vast number of youth scouts covering the whole of the UK. We had to have interpreters present for the South American contingent, who followed the conversations through headphones.

I was not actually employed by Manchester City anymore, that had changed a few years ago, I was now part of 'City Football Group'. This means that whilst I can still only work for one team in the Premiership (just like all other scouts) I could effectively be contracted out to work for other teams within the group.

Scouting for City Football Group is like scouting for no other club and at the outset of this development, it meant that I was on a brand-new learning experience.

At any given day or time I would get my game allocated to me, in the main, by Alan Watson but sometimes others, to go and watch a game and look at a player that might be suitable for say, Australia and Melbourne City, perhaps a left full back playing for Bradford, I could be asked to do the same for New York City and the other teams within the group. Essentially, you must have a good knowledge of a wide range of leagues, including the Premiership of course, to be able to recommend a player who will strengthen that particular squad. No other club, that I am aware of, requires this level of knowledge from their scouts.

In addition to all these different caps I was being asked to wear, sometimes more than one at a given game, I also was involved in watching our players who were out on loan at another club, to see how they are doing. Such as Aaron Mooy who we sent out on loan to Huddersfield a few years ago having brought him in from Melbourne City on a free. He was influential in their promotion to the Premiership and whilst my reports were positive, I concluded that he could play in the lower echelons of the Premiership or move back to Australia or even be suitable for New York City in the MLS both our sister clubs. If he was going to stay in England, I recommended we obtain a fee in the region of £10m.

This is the exact fee we received from Huddersfield following their promotion to the Premiership, he is an integral part of the team that is continually fighting against relegation since their promotion.

I must also mention Fergal Harkin, an Irish lad that I have a lot of time for, he has looked after the loan players and regularly gives me feedback on what I have said and what has been conveyed to the player that I have reported on. He's always been complimentary and it gives me a confidence boost when I hear from him. Good to know someone like Fergal thinks I am doing a good job. Even after all this time I still need to be reminded, it stops me getting complacent.

Fergal Harkin and myself.

The other main area as a scout was looking at the younger players emerging in the lower leagues to see if there is potential for development onto our books. For either a career at Manchester City (which to be honest is very rare) or to bring them in and develop them to sell on, again quite a tall order. It's getting harder and harder to find players at a reasonable price to bring into City Football Group.

Hopefully that explains what are now the main areas that I cover since not being involved in team match reports; when I was full time covering Europe for match reports on opponents for our Champions League and player recruitment in places such as Serbia, Romania, Poland, Germany, Spain, Holland, etc.

However, nothing ever stands still in scouting and the club has re-structured again, this time having specialist groups, concentrating on goalkeepers, Europe, loan players we send out to other clubs, youth, USA, Australia etc.

So, whilst I was not so heavily involved, I would still get sent to watch players in the above categories from time to time as well as my main area which was reporting on young players for development purposes. One weekend (No. 2018) I was watching a goalkeeper, two young players emerging in the Championship and one of our player's currently on loan, who were all playing in the same game. So, three different hats, with the addition to outfield players playing in respective positions. As player reports have areas that are position specific, for example a number 9 a striker, has different qualities or characteristics to a number 6 who is a holding midfielder, who in turn is different to a number 2, who is a right back.

Complicated?

You should have been to the meeting when it was launched a few years ago!

From this, you can see that club scouts have to be versatile and assess not only different levels of ability but the different characteristics for those players.

It makes life interesting to say the least!

Pitch invasion for all the right reasons having just won the Premier League for the second time beating West Ham on the 11th of May 2014, 2-0.

	GD	Points
City	+65	86
Liverpool	+51	84
Chelsea	+44	82

Season's between 2014 & 2016

The next couple of seasons were a bit of a come down from the highs that we felt we had been reaching. We had been pushing the boundaries further ever since the takeover, but the rocket that I refer to had stalled again.

Me pictured with Claudia Reyna, Senior official from New York City FC

Me pictured with Kaldoon Al Mubarak Chairman of Manchester City FC

In the following couple of seasons from that closely fought title, we finished 2nd and 4th respectively in the Premier League; only winning the League Cup against Liverpool via penalties in 2016. One thing we could be proud of was our run to the Champions League Semi Final's; losing out to Real Madrid who were in the middle of a period of European domination. Despite winning a trophy, Manuel was sacked on the 30th of June 2016.

During the close of that 2016 season, Lynda and I, decided to take a break in Cyprus. Wherever I seem to go football in some way seems to follow me.

We were sitting by the pool at the hotel, when this below average height young man who was obviously an athlete of some sort came walking past, I said to Lynda "You know his face is familiar."

This went on for a few days. We caught each other glancing at one another and eventually got to the nodding stage of, 'where do I know you from?'

I had noticed that every day he disappeared around mid-morning and went to the Gym, I was still saying to Lynda, "I really know his face."

Eventually, I plucked up the courage to approach him as he finished his morning session in the gym. I said, "Sorry to intrude, but I seem to know you from somewhere and it has been bugging me for days now."

I just started to ramble on, and he said what do you do, I replied "I am a Senior Scout for Manchester City F.C."

He replied "that is probably it then, I am a footballer" he said. It still didn't twig who he was.

He then said, "I play for Everton, my name is Aaron Lennon." To say I was embarrassed goes without saying, I then started to ramble on again. "I should know your face I have done reports on you; very positive I may add."

He told me he nearly signed for MCFC, but the deal fell through on terms etc. I went on to briefly say to him, I cover not just the UK but look for players for Melbourne City and New York City, in a few years you could do a job in the MLS for New York City.

He seemed interested and said that could well be a good option for him in a few years.

I closed the conversation down by saying, "I know you value your privacy, and I won't disturb you again." He seemed pleased that he could get on with his holiday and I was not going to blow his cover.

We saw him and his girlfriend from time to time but I kept my word and left him alone, we did however bump into him in the Hotel A La Carte restaurant as they were on the next table, so we had a brief discussion before we went our separate ways, I wished him all the best for the coming season and if he needed a testimonial as to how hard he was working on his fitness during the close season, he had my name just contact Manchester City.

To say I was sorry to hear that not so long after that he was ill suffering from stress related symptoms, again goes without saying. I contacted Everton and asked my contact there to pass on my best wishes and hope he makes a full recovery.

I was very pleased that things seem to have gone well for him when he got a move to Burnley. He seems to have turned the corner and is back playing first team football.

This isn't just the one occasion this has happened over the years there have been many other occasions, such as chance meetings with Emelyn Hughes on a plane to Tenerife; George Graham in Dubai at the Ritz Carlton; John Aldridge ex Liverpool player in a restaurant in Portugal, along with others.

8

THE PEP TALK

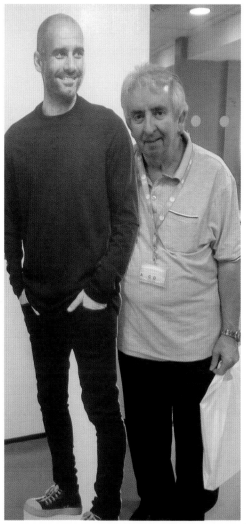

Season – 2016/17

The well-respected Pep Guardiola was appointed manager on 1st July 2016. Whilst we were now regarded as a main player, success was still hard to achieve, as Pep put his stamp on the team. We won nothing.

Questions were being asked about Pep, was he as good as people thought?

I go back to the first meeting in August 2016 where Pep came and gave a talk to the global scouts meeting and he left his mark on everyone at that meeting, there was no doubt in my mind he was the 'real deal', all he needed was time to get the squad he wanted and to mould those players into his way of playing. This was going to take time.

He spent over an hour and a half with the scouts, giving us what he wanted, how we could achieve it and answered question after question with absolute confidence, which in turn rubbed off on his audience.

There were so many things that I took away from that meeting, but he used a white board with magnetic discs to show how he wanted to play and how he would look to retain possession. In his first season this was questioned by the media, However, I was certain in the coming season 2017 to 2018 this would be achieved.

At that first meeting in August he spent a lot of time explaining things, but one thing really stood out was 'possession was key'. If we have the ball they can't score, if we restrict the opposition getting on the ball, we restrict their opportunities to score. He wanted a minimum of 70% possession and we regularly achieve that now and certainly did in his second season 2017 to 2018.

I recall just before he departed that first meeting, he summarised everything he said and what he expected from us. It went something along the following lines:

"I have explained what my philosophy of football is. I have told you what I expect, from everyone in this room, I have told you the sort of players I want and need to achieve our goals and objectives."

I recall the following word for word, which was one of those moments that the hair stands up on the back of your neck. He stood behind me with his hand on my left shoulder speaking to everyone in the room.

"You people, as scouts for Manchester City are the most important people within this club, make no mistake, our future success for this club from what I have said to you relies on everyone in this room driving this club forward. Let no one tell you otherwise."

You could hear a pin drop, my hair was bristling on the back of my neck, everyone was mesmerised, that was when I knew we were onto something special.

I think Pep realised he had left people not knowing what to say, he quickly added (tongue in cheek), "If you don't deliver, I kill you all", his audience laughed and applauded his contribution at the same time.

The rocket was about to go into supercharge. We started the new season brilliantly going unbeaten. However, we were bought back down to earth with a great big thud!

Our rocket had faltered yet again. We dropped out of the League Cup in the fourth round, the FA Cup in the Semi Finals; losing to eventual winners Arsenal, and the Last 16 in Europe. Chelsea and Spurs finished 15 and eight points above us respectively as we had to settle for 3rd in the league.

A big summer lay ahead of us.

Season – 2017/18

At the start of the season, the pressure was on from the outset. Little did we know what was about to happen. We were about to send the rocket higher and faster than ever had been achieved by anyone before! Prepare the ship - Warp Factor 9 - we were about to take off.

In previous pages, I have made the following comment.

Can things get any better? – Well, they did.

This season was make or break in my opinion. There was no hiding place. All the talk, the hype when Pep arrived, only for that first season in charge to result in no silverware - this could not happen again.

Our season could not have started much better. We went unbeaten in all competitions, until the last matchday in the Champions League where we took a rotated team to Shakhtar and lost 2-1. Before then, we had not dropped a point in the Champions League and were midway through a colossal 18 league match winning streak and 22-match unbeaten league run. A monumental start. This included results such as crucial victories at Old Trafford (2-1) & Stamford Bridge (1-0) as well as titanic victories against Liverpool, Crystal Palace (both 5-0) & Stoke (7-2) at home, plus a crushing win over Watford away from home (6-0). Bookmakers were paying out as early as December, but we still had work to do.

The unbeaten league run came to an end when we went to Anfield and lost a mouth-watering game 4-3. As much as this hurt, it wasn't going to get in our way of winning back that Premier League trophy. Our FA Cup run had started positively as well and with that came talk of an elusive quadruple. Something that no team had ever done before. A League Cup final was secured after we triumphed twice over a spirited Bristol City side that had knocked the holders and our neighbours out in the last round. The final would be played against Arsene Wenger's Arsenal in what would be his last final as Arsenal boss. Unfortunately, the Monday before that game had seen us come up against Wigan Athletic in the FA Cup 5th round who ended any hopes of a domestic treble and trophy quadruple. We lost 1-0 but knew all was not lost. A final now in front of us, we were desperate for that first trophy under Pep. Thankfully, we did the job and won 3-0. This was just the beginning of what Pep had been trying to create.

With his relentless nature for success, Pep was determined not to let anyone get complacent. This led to a week where we had two legs against Liverpool to secure a Champions League Semi Final spot and an opportunity to secure the title the earliest anyone had ever been able to before. It couldn't have been setup any better, as United were the visitors to the Etihad that day. The first leg of that Quarter Final tie will be remembered more for the Liverpool fans swarming our coach and throwing objects at it as we arrived. Had we not been shaken by that; the outcome of a 3-0 defeat could have been so different.

The weekend arrived for the Manchester derby that would decide whether we won the title or not. At half time we were 2-0 up and cruising towards the title. Whether that got to their heads, I don't know but in the second half we collapsed and lost 3-2. The loss to Liverpool hurt, but not as much as that loss against United having been 2-0 up. We had another leg against Liverpool, to resurrect what happened the week before. The Etihad was rocking and ready for action. After two minutes, we were ahead! The decibels seemed to get louder and louder. Liverpool somehow held on until half time. Aggregate at half time read 1-3. We'd seen Barcelona come back from being 4-0 down last season so we were confident that another goal would lead to another and another just like when we played them earlier in the season. However, Salah silenced us with a goal around ten minutes into the second half and then Firmino finished us off later in the game. Liverpool progressed with a 5-1 aggregate victory. We were absolutely devastated. The dreams of a Champions League Semi Final and Premier League title in the same week evaporated. In the league, we had the chance to secure the title again at the weekend, but for European glory, we had another season in the offing before we could have another crack at that trophy. All our eggs went into the league basket now with records still possible.

We travelled to Wembley now with the memories of the League Cup victory still fresh in our minds. We couldn't postpone this title any longer, could we? We won 3-1. The Premier League had returned to the Etihad. Pep says he knew we would be champions after 15 minutes of the game because unlike the Liverpool & United games, we continued to create chances even when being pegged back by Spurs. I wish I'd been told he'd said that as I'm a terrible watcher of us.

Five games remained in the season; Swansea, West Ham, Huddersfield, Brighton & Southampton. We needed 13 points to be the first team to secure a century of points in a single league season, three wins to achieve the most ever in a season and with those wins & lots of goals, other achievements were also possible. We beat Swansea, West Ham & Brighton, but only managed a draw with Huddersfield. We needed a victory over Southampton to take 100 points from a single league season. To say we left it late is an understatement. Gabriel Jesus netted in the 94th minute of the match to secure our status in Premier League history as the greatest team. The records came with that, most goals (106), most wins (32), most points (100), best goal difference (+79), biggest margin of victory for a title (19 points).

Manchester City record breaking league title victory 2017/18

Won	32
Goal difference	+79
Points	100

Everything that had been discussed at that first meeting with Pep had finally been delivered with interest. It was regarded, in many quarters, that season 2017/18 had seen the best football ever played in the Premiership. We'd dominated it from start to finish with many of the objectives Pep had set, delivered game after game. In short, we were on another planet.

When you compare this season to our first title, it was a million miles away from that late great goal from Aguerooooooooooooooo to pip United on goal difference to the title.

Could things get any better? Well…

Season – 2018/19

In many respects ironically, this season has been my quietest season since I started scouting which has given me time to reflect on what more I have to offer Manchester City.

My workload had diminished, and I now concentrate on what was labelled Emerging Talent. This is young players between 17 and say 20 breaking through into the first team of clubs not only in the Premiership, but mainly the divisions below. We as a club, do not miss many players that come through and our owners would expect us to know about future rising stars like Daniel James for example.

If we did, they would ask questions, "Why do we have no reports on such youngsters, with the scouting and recruitment system we have in place?"

I would add that most young players coming through that I have reported on will get a 'D' and are often at their level, but you must watch them as there is the occasional gem out there.

In terms of the football on the pitch, Pep and the boys were performing very well again. We'd beaten Chelsea in the Community Shield to start the season well and give us some momentum heading into the early part of the season.

	Won	GD	Points
City	32	+72	98
Liverpool	30	+67	97

In the league this season, we were pushed all the way by an energetic Liverpool side that just seemed incapable of dropping points at one stage in the season. We were seven points adrift of them when it came to the 3rd of January 2019. If we lost or even dropped points, that would have made the task twice as hard as it was already. The fact we'd had a chance to beat them at Anfield late on, earlier in the season and not taken it was a wrong we had to right. Prior to that game, we had lost three of our last five and Liverpool were unbeaten in the league up until that point. It was a closely fought encounter and thankfully, we found ourselves on the right side of a 2-1 victory. After that game, we only dropped three points in the remaining 17 fixtures whereas, Liverpool dropped a further eight points which proved to be decisive in our quest for back to back Premier League trophies. Arguably, the most iconic moment in our season will be when exiting captain and defensive stalwart, Vincent Kompany, hit an absolute rocket past Kasper Schmeichel in our penultimate game, to edge past Leicester by a goal to nil. The final game against Brighton we went behind, but that was enough to kick us in to gear as we went on to win 4-1 and retain our crown.

The great thing about this City team is they're never satisfied. They always want more. In the League Cup, we stormed our way to the final demolishing a Burton side in the Semi Final 10-0 on aggregate; a record for the competition. In the final, we edged past Chelsea via penalties. The game in general will be remembered for the Kepa-Sarri incident where Kepa refused to be subbed, but our players kept their heads amongst all the madness to see off the Blues 4-3 on penalties.

Meanwhile, in the FA Cup, we saw off a few potential upsets, particularly Swansea who were 2-0 up at half time. Thankfully, down to Sterling & Aguero, we fought back, another great characteristic of this City side; to progress to the Semi Finals. For the second time at

Wembley in a cup competition, we looked unconvincing edging out Brighton 1-0. What was to happen in the final though was simply stunning.

We were facing a Watford side that we had taken six points off during the season in the league. That sounds like we made it easy, but it was far more hard work than I can describe. Watford are a side that never give up (like us). They were down and out in the Semi Finals before an inspired performance by a former Barcelona youngster Gerard Deulofeu who turned a game that Wolves were dominating 2-0 with 20 minutes to go, into a 3-2 victory for Watford after extra time. This was not going to be easy. At half time we were cruising 2-0, but Watford were showing signs of fighting back again. Pep sent Kevin de Bruyne on and he scored our third goal and assisted our fourth to really kill the game off. Sterling added a couple to make it 6-0 which certainly didn't tell the whole story. In history though, we now share a record with Bury for the biggest victory in the FA Cup final and are the only team in England to complete the domestic treble. It was an exceptional season.

I can't help but think about that VAR decision, that disallowed a goal (and rightly so) against Spurs that would have sent us through to the Champions League Semi Final. It was a cruel way to go out, but at the end of the day, it wasn't meant to be. It hurts more as I enter the retirement phase of my career as a scout, but I'm sure we will break that European Cup duck sooner rather than later.

Me with the Hall of Silver

9

MY GUIDE TO SCOUTING

Structured Approach to Reports

I have come full circle, so I am going to return to the beginning and expand on how I developed reports. I will talk about the forms I used to prepare the final document. You must bear in mind that player reports differ from opposing match reports which is a different discipline altogether.

At this point I would like to say that football is all about opinions, therefore my opinion outlined in what is to follow does not necessarily represent the views and opinions of the clubs I have worked for.

When I started with Fulham, I basically had a blank canvas to work upon and develop, I was sent a few forms in the post with no instructions, just do what you think is right. These forms were the templates I used to develop myself as well as improve the quality of the reports.

I feel that my career in banking helped me, as a structured approach is also required in that environment as well.

I will be mixing stories with advice I have been given and advice that I would give to an aspiring scout.

Scunthorpe Utd v Grimsby Town

I was sent to Scunthorpe Utd, to do a match report on Grimsby Town when I was working for Fulham. Because it is a local derby, it was nearly a sell-out. I had a seat near the halfway line near the Director's box, which was full. I was in with the Scunthorpe supporters.

As the game kicked off, I could feel the eyes of people around me wondering what I was doing. One after another I could hear them saying

"Who is he?"

"What is he doing?"

Just before half time, the old boy next to me asked,

"Are you with Grimsby?"

"No" I replied. He passed it on down the line to my right.

"Are you with Scunthorpe press then?"

"No" I told him again. He passed it on down the line.

"Who are you then?"

At this point, I put him out of his misery. We reached half time and of course some wanted to chat. He asked for my thoughts, I really did not say much; except I thought the winger on the opposite side will be dangerous and he looks capable of causing problems. Within minutes of the kick-off, the winger did exactly what I had predicted, pure luck on my part.

The old boy stood up (we were yards from the dugout) and he shouted to the Scunthorpe manager (his name will remain secret),

"If this scout can see the danger - why don't you give him your job?"

I kept my head down and carried on with my report.

Player Report Process

I decided to get to games at least one hour before kick-off.

This enabled me to have a look at the warm-up. It was especially useful when assessing goalkeepers. I was able to observe his kicking style, which foot he preferred and whether he kicked it high or flat; did he stay on his line for crosses, whether he was a shot stopper, what his agility was like and was he better diving to his left or down to his right.

When assessing an outfield player, you could use the time to obtain information that would help you identify him in the game such as hair colour, boot colour etc.

This procedure I developed, and it proved very useful over the years.

At kick off, the first and vital job was to get the formation for both sides. I set myself a target of getting all formations done within the first 5 minutes. The next vital job was to get the strongest foot identified for the player or players, being assessed as potential transfer targets.

I developed a form to collate information for players, from both the home and away side. From there I could start to develop the report for players. Depending on how many I was watching would determine how detailed the report would be.

If I was watching one player, I would follow him both on and off the ball, players in different positions have different strengths and weaknesses. I would make notes such as his ability with both feet (or not, as the case may be), his pace, his agility, his approximate height (this could be checked later, but I found it a good exercise to try and gauge it myself; it helped focus the mind). A winger has different attributes from a centre back and so on. This style of report developed continually as the years went by. The report would be based on whether the player being observed was better than what we had already. If he was not, then he would not really improve our squad. Over the years, the information that is required has changed from fairly basic to a very characteristic position specific.

The terminology for positions has changed as well. A right back, for example, is now known as a 2A, a right centre back is now a 3A and so on across the back, or block as it is now categorised, due to the number of foreign Managers in the game.

A central midfield player who plays deep is now known as a number 6. Whilst a right footed player playing on the right is a winger or number 7 and playing on the left as a right footer, he would be a number 11.

Confused? I was at the beginning.

When this was launched to all the Scouts at a meeting some years ago, one scout at Manchester City who will remain nameless sitting next to me looking perplexed, bearing in mind that clubs now use squad numbers that go into double figure's such as Fernandinho wears number 25, Jesus wears number 33 etc., turned to me and said, "what f***ing position to put them down for?" He had not grasped the concept, but he soon understood when I explained the basis of the 2A, 3A etc. (just ignore the squad number).

To say we had a good laugh about it, he just had a mental block due to the amount of information we were having to digest at these scouts' meetings.

Returning to the early reports at Fulham, the reports were done by hand and faxed to Fulham by 12noon on the Sunday from games observed on the Saturday. It would be the same for midweek games that I had watched the previous evening; 12noon the next day. When it was a full match report this meant that I had to be up early around 6am to get the bulk of the report done, as I had a full-time job as a Regional Manager for NatWest Bank.

The manner and development kept evolving to what we have now,

PLAYER ASSESSMENT FORM

N	A	F	Comments **Home**	R	N	A	F	Comments **Away**	R
Pitch Condition								**Weather**	

Individuals who stand out.			

Name MICHAEL DAWSON	Club NOTTINGHAM FOREST	Position CENTRAL DEFENDER		Report Number
Height 6 FT 2 INCH	Age/D.O.B. 18 11 1983	Physique GOOD STRONG WELL PROPORTIONED		Nationality
Date 3 28/8 2002 1983	Scout JOHN STARRS	Opposition CHELSEA RES	Venue NOTTINGHAM	
Pitch GOOD TRUE SURFACE	Weather DRY FAIRLY MILD	Score N-C 1 0	Opposition Quality LOOKED VERY YOUNG	

Attribute	Mark	Comments
Right Foot	8½	VERY CLEAN CONTROLLED CUSHIONED TOUCH
Left Foot	6	NOTHING OVER ELABORATE. TAKES TOUCHES.
Temperament	10	SHOULD EXCELLENT ATTITUDE IN ALL CHALLENGES
Control and touch	8½	NEAT TIDY 1ST TOUCH TIGHT - SPACE FOR HIMSELF
Passing	9	AGAIN NEAT WELL WEIGHTED, GOOD RANGE, ACCURATE
Heading	9	ATTACKS BALL WITH PURPOSE, CONVICTION, COMMITMENT
Pace	8½	HAS GOOD LONG STRIDE, FLUID RECOVERS QUICKLY
Work Rate	8	GOES FORWARD SET PIECES, QUICK TO RETURN TO DEF ROLE
Defensive qualities	9	STRONG IN AIR, COMPOSED ON GROUND
Offensive qualities	7	FORWARD ALL SET PIECES, PRESENCE CONSTANT THREAT
Awareness/ Positional sense	9	CONTROLLED, TALKED TO HIS BACK LINE. GOOD VISION
Team Play	8	MAKES SELF AVAILABLE AS OUTLET FOR OTHERS

Additional Notes A YOUNG MAN WHO HAS IMMENSE POTENTIAL, VERY LIGHT ON HIS FEET, HAS MATURITY BEYOND HIS YEARS, HAS GREAT PRESENCE ATTACKED BALL ESPECIALLY IN AIR, • VERY IMPRESSIVE HAVING TAKEN A HEFTY LATE CHALLENGE ON 80 MINS GOT UP NEVER PHASED HIM CONTINUED TO PLAY AS IF NEVER HAPPENED. AN EXCITING PROSPECT SURE TO IMPROVE

Total Mark 100½	Action A STAR IN THE MAKING. WATCH AGAIN VERY SOON.

which is a list of characteristics that suit each position. This is completed directly onto a template, on a system called Scout7; which goes straight into the club's master Scout7 system.

When I was at Fulham, I was only looking for players for the first team to improve the squad (which is the same as the majority of scouts do who work for other clubs).

However, when I moved to Manchester City, whilst the outset was the same, due to the development of City over the years which has grown and grown since the new owners took over some ten years ago, so did my role.

The development and purchase of various clubs worldwide such as New York City FC in the MLS (USA), Melbourne City FC in the A League (Australia), Girona (Spain) where we own a substantial stake in the club, along with clubs in Japan, South America and so on. This meant that technically I no longer work for Manchester City but, for CFG (City Football Group).

Whilst I can still only work for one Premiership Club, I can be used by the other clubs owned within the group.

I am unaware of any other club that has Scouts who undertake such diverse levels of ability for player reports.

This means that at any one game I could, and have reported on potential players for different clubs at different levels, not forgetting the possibility of assessing one of our players, who might be on loan, or a young player under 20 breaking into the first team.

To say this is challenging is an understatement.

To undertake these roles, it means watching games either live on television from the USA, Australia, etc. Why? Because I have to be aware of the standard in each of those countries, or indeed the level of our youth team compared to young players at other clubs. If I am to provide a measured opinion to whether they are suitable for consideration for the respective teams, it's like wearing different caps for different teams, but they are all different caps.

The Wrong Player

In my early days I had a lot to learn, so I was taking things on board at a fast rate. On a cold, freezing Tuesday night Arthur Cox sent me to watch a player called Tony Vaughan, playing for Manchester City reserves, ironically enough I was working for Fulham then.

Anyone who has been to Grimsby in the summer will tell you how cold it is, never mind winter. It was so cold you could see your own breath, so when I was given the opportunity to watch the game from an executive box behind glass, I jumped at the chance.

Team sheets arrived. Tony Vaughan was playing at number 6. I settled down and waited for the kick-off.

I made my notes and headed home at the end of the game. I got up early the next morning, completed the report and sent it off to Fulham. Job done!

I received a telephone call from Arthur later in the week, we exchanged pleasantries before Arthur said "About the report on Tony Vaughan, everything you have said is spot on."

"Oh, that's great." Was my response.

"Shame he was not playing" he replied immediately.

"What!" I exclaimed; I was shocked.

The report I had done was totally accurate for the player who played in the number 6 shirt, but on the way to Grimsby he was bitten by something, and Tony Vaughan's leg started to swell up as they were on the team bus.

"It was a cold night and I bet you watched the game from behind glass?" Arthur went onto say.

"Yes, I did."

"I thought so, you can't hear anything from behind glass, especially the team line ups. I phoned Joe Royle and he told me what had happened"

Suffice to say I felt such a prat!

Arthur then gave me some advice – sit outside and you won't miss anything. I had just received a polite b******ing. It taught me a valuable lesson and it never happened again.

Full Opposition Match Reports

The procedures for starting player reports were the same for opposition match reports, I would get there at least an hour before kick-off and go through the same procedure, to begin to obtain the information required which at times could end up as a 24 page document, providing a full team analysis, compared to a one page document for a player report.

The difference now was instead of focusing on one or two players, I had to focus on all eleven.

In addition I was not focusing on whether a player would be suitable for us as a transfer potential, but on their role within the team and their strengths so as we could nullify them or indeed their weaknesses so as we could exploit them as individuals, a different perspective totally than a player assessment.

TEAM ASSESSMENT FORM

Num	Name	FOOT	H/P	COMTS. G/K	L/R		R

I developed a form that could be used to collect appropriate information such as squad number height left foot/right foot, or on occasions which is rare, both feet.

This turned into effectively short pen pictures of each player, including any subs that were used, who they replaced and when.

As I have said these team reports are far more technical and detailed, in that the formation diagrams also include the shape in transition from attack to defence and vice versa, how do they play, e.g. long ball or play out from the back, do they have a target man.

The most difficult aspect of diagrams was attacking corners and free kicks, I had to put all ten outfield players onto a diagram and draw lines, showing movement taker of the corner etc.

This was particularly important if the team being reported upon were set piece specialists.

When all was virtually complete, I had to summarise in a short section entitled "how to expose the opposition." In short, give my opinion as to how to nullify them and win the game.

I am sure you can see how much more complicated match reports are compared to player reports.

That's why it takes over four hours or so to complete match reports, as opposed to around 20 minutes for a player report.

But in the end, if I had spotted even the slightest area to concentrate on that made the difference between winning and losing, I had done my job. When I watched games, I was a bag of nerves shouting at the television giving instructions such as keep him on his weaker foot, don't let him run in to there, pick him up at corners etc.

Lynda always said, "They can't hear you." But it never stopped me as I knew what was coming, I kicked and headed every ball, by the time the game was over I was knackered!

It was always a good weekend when I had a part to play having completed a report that ended with us getting a result, especially if I had done the last report of the three (every opposition was scouted three times prior to when we played them). It was even better when I had done all three reports on an opposition prior to the match, like I did when I compiled the three reports on M********* United before we played them, the season we won the Premiership for the first time in 2012. It was even more satisfying, as United never had a shot on target when we played them; we won 1-0 with a headed goal by Vincent Kompany. It went a long way to us winning the title, in fact we would not have won the title had we lost or drawn that game.

Derby County v Ipswich Town

I was given a match report to do on Ipswich Town as Manchester City were playing them the following week, away in the FA Cup.

I got there, at least 90 minutes before kick-off, to prepare and get organised, I picked up my ticket and as normal, Derby had allocated me a Director's Box seat on the halfway line, which is spot on for doing match reports.

I went to the Executive Lounge and purchased an orange juice from the bar and as I turned around, I saw Kevin Keegan coming into the lounge. He saw me and made his way over, I asked him what he was doing there.

"We thought we would take the game in, as we don't play until tomorrow,"

I asked who 'we' was?

"Arthur is over there." Kevin answered.

As we got to Arthur and said hello, I then asked them if they were doing the report instead of me. Kevin replied, "Oh no, you're doing it"

Kevin went on to say that he had arranged for Arthur to sit on one side of me and he would sit on the other. I looked at him in horror and said in a shocked tone "You are joking!" He then started to tease me, saying we are going to watch how you gather information, how you deal with set pieces, and most of all what the report looks like that you're going to submit against what we think.

Then an elderly lady approached Kevin and asked if he would sign her programme, as always Kevin was obliging and proceeded to sign it, asking her name to make it more personal. As he was signing it, he said "can I introduce John he is one of our scouts."

As I held out my hand to shake her hand Kevin said, "You would not think to look at him, but he often claims expenses for games but never turns up, we came today to catch him out"

I was gradually going red and getting worse the more Kevin said. She looked at me in a disapproving manner, but then said, "Surely not", but who was she going to believe, me or Kevin Keegan?

To say he was making me very nervous, well it's difficult to put into words. As the game kicked off, I was very conscious of them both. I need not have worried, they both let me get on with the job and never made a single note between them.

They left some 20 minutes before the end; I waited a further 10 minutes before making my exit as usual to avoid the traffic. It's normal practice for scouts to leave early as you may have a long journey home and sitting in a queue for an hour is no fun. Basically, when you see a mass exodus around the 80-minute mark, it's probably just the scouts getting away.

The philosophy being that if you have not got what you need in the first 80 minutes, you won't get it in the last 10.

Following these match reports, the FA Cup game was played between Ipswich & City with City winning 4-1. I was told later that I had been very good under pressure. Another part of the learning curve successfully completed.

Dream Squad

Over the years people always ask me who is the best player you have ever discovered or recommended.

I always reply, with the worldwide coverage these days, it's not about discovering a player as they are out there for all to see.

It's about looking deeper than that, it's about looking at their attitude, work rate on and off the ball, body language etc. I once gave a player 'D' who is valued at nearly £200 Million. Why? Because he would, in my opinion, disrupt the dressing room and that was in 2012.

Whilst he has done well, he has had his moments and is still having them so in my opinion, he's not worth the risk. It is sometimes more about who you don't recommend, and not who you do recommend. It's about ignoring reputations.

It's also difficult to quantify players and compare them over the years. In addition, a player back in say, 2001, whom I recommended would not get a recommendation in say 2006. The same goes for a player in 2012, would not get a recommendation now in 2019. And so on.

To build a team, you must always look to improve and strengthen the squad without too much disruption. A great example was Pablo Zabaleta, a stalwart of the Manchester City first team at number 2A (right back). He was never a weak link, but his position became exposed at times, so it had to be changed. Pablo is still in the Premiership with West Ham and starting regularly, and of course Joe Hart became surplus to requirements.

I always try to explain, that when I first started scouting at both Fulham, and then Manchester City from 2001 onwards, looking for players the window of opportunity to find players, was as wide and as long as a football pitch. However, as teams develop and keep improving like Manchester City's have since 2001/02, the window of opportunity to find players better than we already have, has become smaller.

Now in 2019, I would say that the window is no bigger and has become as narrow as the six-yard box, and the window is getting smaller and smaller as each season, we grow stronger and stronger. I hope that paints a picture for you.

I would like to point out at this stage, any recommendations that I made over the years are my opinion and do not reflect the opinions of either Fulham or Manchester City. They are mine and mine alone.

I would also point out, that the players recommended were assessed at the time they were playing and would probably not get the same recommendation, as the quality has developed over the years. Therefore, they're included in my Dream Squad as I have no other players to call upon that I have scouted.

So here we go.

GOALKEEPERS (Number 1)

JOE HART (Born April 1987)

I watched Joe once playing for Shrewsbury Town at Boston United and sent a recommendation. We signed him for £600,000; absolute bargain! He became an essential part of the team, playing a major part in winning the first two trophies in 2011 and 2012 - the FA Cup and Premier league title respectively. He also went on to be England's number one.

SERGIO ROMERO (Born February 1982)

On a trip to Holland, I saw him play for AZ Alkmaar. He kept a clean sheet and saved a penalty when they were 5-0 up. He looked determined not to concede, He went on to join Sampdoria, Monaco and is now the number two at M******** United. Since I recommended him, he has gone on to win 96 International Caps for Argentina.

JACK BUTLAND (Born March 1993)

Saw him first in 2012 at the age of 19. Said that he has the potential to be another Joe Hart, a great shot stopper.

DEFENDERS (2A, 3A, 4A & 5A)

KYLE WALKER (Born May 1990)

Saw him playing for Sheffield United between 2007 and 2008, before he signed for Spurs. We purchased him from Spurs for a fee said to be around £50 Million a few years later in 2017. He is now the regular at right back (2A).

JOHN STONES (Born May 1994)

First time I saw him he was playing for Barnsley at Leeds United as

a right back. I thought straight away he would be better suited as a 3a (Right Centre Back).

I gave him an 'A' on more than one occasion after that, and strongly recommended we sign him. Everton got in first and bought him for a fee reported to be £3 Million in 2013. He developed and we stepped in and bought him for a fee in and around £50 million with add-ons.

He has been a regular in and around a very competitive squad, and I feel we have still to see the best of him. He has won 38 International caps for England.

Probably my best pic with Joe Hart (See photo previous page).

STEFAN SAVIC (Born January 1991)

Spotted him between 2010 and 2011 playing for Partizan. MCFC signed him for £6 Million. He never really settled into the Premiership, although he was part of the squad that won the Premiership in 2012 making enough appearances to get a winner's medal. I always felt that we pushed him too early and he needed more time to adjust. However, we sold him to Fiorentina in 2012.

He became a steady and reliable player before moving to Atletico Madrid for €10 Million.

He has Currently played over 86 games for Atletico Madrid since 2015 and is a regular for Montenegro. I can't help feeling had we waited and given him time to develop, he might well have been another solid player for us in the block (Defence) even as a squad player.

FABIAN DELPH (BORN November 1989)

Watched him during the season 2014/2015 playing for Aston Villa, especially towards the end of the season when Aston Villa were struggling to avoid relegation. He impressed me with his all-round enterprise, leadership and work rate/commitment. Whilst I felt that he would not be a regular starter, more of a squad player I believed he could well be an asset. We bought him on the 17th July 2015 for £8 Million. My predictions have I feel, been correct especially filling in at 5A (Left Back). He has proved to be what I predicted and more. Shown a team player attitude, doing a job when called upon. £8 Million well spent. He has also won 18 full international caps.

He can also double up in midfield as a Holding Number 6 with his versatility.

MICHAEL DAWSON (Born November 1983)

I first saw Michael playing for Nottingham Forest reserves on the 28th March 2002. I gave a very positive report against Chelsea Reserves, and many more, on many occasions thereafter, however we never did sign him and he went on to play for Spurs following his transfer to them in 2005 for £8 Million. I predicted following that first report that he was a star in the making. He went on to play for Spurs until before being transferred to Hull City in the August of 2014, he is back where he started at Nottingham Forest following a transfer to them in May 2018. Due to illness and injury over the years his International caps have been limited.

NATHAN AKE (Born February 1995)

I went to Holland to watch a couple of games in April 2010. Including an under 15's game between Holland and Ireland. This boy stood out technically, physically and ability wise from the kick-off. First impression was, he looked the part and was the double of Ruud Gullit in all departments. He did not disappoint in his performance; I came back waxing lyrical about the boy and said without question we must sign him without delay before he is snapped up by someone else. However, he had his heart on signing for Chelsea where his hero

Ruud Gullit was involved. He agreed to join Chelsea in 2011 at the age of 16 from Feyenoord. Following several loan spells, he eventually was transferred in 2017 to Bournemouth, for a fee of around £20 Million. Whilst he is a left-sided centre back as a preferred position, he is also not out of place as a 5A (left back) or indeed a 6 (holding player).

This trip was also memorable for getting stuck in Amsterdam, following the Iceland volcano eruption that closed Airports across Europe. I suppose there are worse places to be stranded. I eventually got home via the Eurostar train.

PHIL JAGIELKA (Born August 1982)

Recommended around 2002 whilst playing for Sheffield United, he moved to Everton in 2007 for a fee of around £4 Million. He was born in Manchester so would have been a good addition to our squad at the time.

HOLDING DEFENSIVE MIDFIELDER (Number 6)

N'GOLO KANTE (Born March 1991)

Saw him for the first and only time in the season 2015/2016 when Leicester City won the Premiership against all odds. It was in January 2016 against Stoke City. He was outstanding, a diminutive figure who ran the show. I not only gave him an 'A', but I also followed it up with one of the strongest recommendations I feel I have ever given. I felt he would be ideal as an alternative to Fernandinho as a number 6. He was so impressive, I felt at times that there were two of him.

He would do something, I would look down to write it on my notes, when I looked back in seconds, I could not find him as he was on the other side of the field. I remember thinking that they had three central midfield players, Kante on the right someone in the centre and Kante on the left!

I continued to monitor his progress for the remainder of the season, and I have no doubt he was the difference that made them Champions. Chelsea stepped in for him, after his one and only season with Leicester in the July and bought him for £30 million.

The following season 2016/2017 Chelsea won the league title with 93 points, Spurs were second on 86 points and Manchester City was way back on 78 points. Kante had made the difference I predicted he would, which was no consolation.

He is still playing and calling the shots for Chelsea.

SANDRO (Born March 1989)

He was the other player I picked up on my trip to Venezuela in February 2009 at the Sud America under 20's. He was a strong solid player who technically was very good. He was eventually signed by Spurs (not again) for a fee in the region of £6 Million from Internacional where a partnership agreement had been struck between the two clubs.

He played 81 games for Spurs and made 17 full international appearances for Brazil between 2009 and 2012. His career was dogged by regular injuries, which curtailed him having a much more illustrious career. He is currently on loan at Udinese in what must be considered as the twilight of his career.

WIDE MEN (Number 7 or 11)

SHAUN WRIGHT-PHILLIPS (Born October 1981)

I started scouting in 1998 with Fulham and it's ironic that one of my early recommendations was in the October of year 2000. I recommended that we should monitor this boy very closely, he was playing for Manchester City reserves away at Sheffield Wednesday. The reports in those days were not as comprehensive as they are today.

Shaun caught my eye from the kick-off. His pace, diminutive build, his enthusiasm on a cold night in Sheffield being watched by nearly one man and a dog, plus me.

I suggested to Fulham that they watch him closely. On this occasion I was pleased that nothing came of my recommendation and Shaun stayed with Manchester City, especially when I joined City from Fulham not long after that. I recall giving him marks out of 10 and on one category I gave him 0, which affected his overall total. That category was Heading, no surprise as he was only 5ft 5 inches.

The rest is history as they say. Kevin Keegan worked hard with him on his final ball as I have mentioned in a previous chapter and Shaun grew and grew, but we were a selling club in those days and could not turn down an offer of around £20 million for him from Chelsea.

He never reached the heights at Chelsea, as I felt he was a confident player and never held down a first team place week in week out. He returned to Manchester City in August 2008 for a fee of around £8.5 Million, but again never reached the heights previously under Kevin.

We sold him to Queens Park Rangers in 2011 for an undisclosed fee. He is still held in high regard by staff and supporters alike not just because of his football prowess, but he is a really nice man and I have no hesitation in putting him in my team. He acquired 36 International caps in his career, a long way from a cold October night in Sheffield in the year 2000.

DOUGLAS COSTA (Born September 1990)

I was asked to cover the Sud America U20 tournament in Venezuela in Feb 2009. The duration of the tournament was over a two-week period. I started with a blank sheet of paper eliminating players to narrow it down after every game. It was like a funnel putting 200 or so players in at the top and filtering them after every game and reducing the players being watched.

In the end, I narrowed it down to two. Sandro who shortly afterwards signed for Spurs (I should have worked for them based on the number of players I suggested that they signed !)

The other was Douglas Costa, he in my opinion was the player of the tournament by an absolute mile. I came back from South America waxing lyrical about this lightly built, young boy around 5ft 8 inch, he had all the hallmarks to be a star in the making, especially with a sweet left foot.

Following the tournament, he signed for Shakhtar Donetsk in 2010 before moving on to Bayern Munich in 2015, then onto Juventus in 2017. Where he still plays.

MATTHEW ETHERINGTON (Born August 1981)

Another wide player who started his career with Peterborough United. His career mirrored that of Simon Davies in the early days and I scouted him for Fulham at the same time as Simon Davies.

Guess what... he joined Spurs at the same time as Simon, in the same deal. He went onto play 45 games for Spurs before moving on. He never really hit the heights he was expected to make and never won a full International cap. He finished his career playing for Stoke City in 2014.

SIMON DAVIES (Born October 1979)

A wide player with quality, who I saw playing for Peterborough

United very early in my scouting career with Fulham. He was at his best as a wide player with balance and pace. He signed for (yes again Spurs) and made his debut on the 9th April 2000.He went on to play 121 games for Spurs, before moving to Everton in 2005. A solid winger who caused many defences problems.

He went on to play 58 times for Wales at senior level.

CENTRAL MIDFIELD ATTACKING (NUMBER 8)

JAMES MADDISON (Born November 1996)

First saw this boy playing for Coventry City in 2015, when he came on as a substitute on 68 minutes.

I would normally ignore making a recommendation based on so little time on the pitch however, he made such an impact as an 18-year-old. I followed him and saw him 4 more times, twice before he signed for Norwich, when I gave him a strong 'B', then twice whilst at Norwich City. I gave an 'A' on both of those occasions; the last time in April 2018 against Cardiff.

He was transferred to Leicester City on the 20th June 2018 for a fee said to be around £22 million.

I predicted he would move to the Premiership and I also believe he has a great future and career ahead of him and is already in my opinion worth twice what Leicester paid for him. Keep a close eye on him, he has the versatility to play as a Number 10 and even as a Number 6 from time to time. He is a star in the making providing he keeps his feet on the ground.

ALBERTO AQUILANI (Born July 1984)

He was recommended following his performances in an under 16's tournament held in Sheffield and surrounding areas around 2001.

He went on to play for Liverpool but was not a success, also Juventus, Milan & Fiorentina among others. Won 38 full International caps for Italy between 2006 and 2014.

Currently a free agent at the age of 34.

CENTRAL MIDFIELD ATTACKING (NUMBER 10)

ISCO (Born April 1992)

Having watched Isco on a video on 18th September 2012 and gave him a strong 'A' with a recommendation that he be followed up live as soon as possible, I was asked to go to Malaga and watch him live on the 29th September 2012.

I flew in and out of Malaga on the same day, having again seen him give a first-class performance. I again gave him an 'A', for me to give him two consecutive 'A' ratings was unheard of. I also said that we should make every effort to sign him.

He was linked to us and Manuel Pellegrini did try to sign him, but Isco chose to join Real Madrid for a fee of around €30 Million. He has won over 34 full international caps and is everything I thought he would be. Another that got away.

NIKO KRANJCAR (Born August 1984)

I picked him up as a youngster playing for Croatia under 16's. He looked a star and had a glittering career especially in England with Portsmouth and Spurs (yes again). He also played for QPR and Glasgow Rangers.

A true professional who never let you down.

He made 81 full International appearances for Croatia.

STRIKER (NUMBER 9A)

ROBERT LEWANDOWSKI (Born August 1988)

I visited Poland in 2008 and whilst he did not play in the game I watched, which was a full International , I got talking to some locals over a couple of days, it's amazing what people tell you as they want to be the one who tells his friends - it was me that told the English Scout about a player.

Well that is exactly what happened, I asked numerous local people who their best young talent was, and the same name kept coming up, so I made a note and we, as a club, picked him up including myself.

He was only 19 when he first came to my attention, and to say he has had an outstanding career in the years to follow would be an understatement. He is a big strong striker, who in 2008 was with Lech Poznan (where we stole the Poznan from after playing them in a European tie, but that's another story).

He eventually moved to Germany playing for Borussia Dortmund in 2010, before a transfer to Bayern Munich in 2014.

We never signed him, and he still plays for Bayern Munich. I don't think he had played a full International when I was first told about him in Poland, but they knew what they were talking about when I look back on those conversations, he has now 104 full International caps to his name.

GIAMPAOLO PAZZINI (Born August 1984)

I saw him in the same tournament as Aquilani. He went on to play for a few clubs including Fiorentina, Sampdoria, both Milan teams among others. He managed to win 25 full International caps between 2009 and 2012.

DEVELOPMENT SQUAD

More recently, I have just been scouting younger players as mentioned earlier. I have a couple of rising stars to tell you about, who I feel have great potential and go on to be worth a lot of money in the coming years.

CHRIS MEPHAM – Defender - Born 5th November 1997

A player who can play in both centre back positions as a number 3A or 4A. He was playing for Brentford last year before joining Bournemouth in the January Window of 2019.

He is 6ft 3 inches tall, a solid athletic frame comfortable in possession. He made his debut as a late substitute in the 4-0 win against Chelsea.

He has a long-term contract and with a fee of around £12 - £15 million reported to have been paid, he can surely only increase in value with experience. He has won 5 full Wales International caps to date.

Keep a close eye on him!

DANIEL JAMES – Winger - Born 10th November 1997

A player I saw playing for Swansea at Rotherham United towards the end of 2018. He caught my eye with his explosive pace and the fact he was comfortable with both feet. He just left defenders in his wake and the well-known phrase sprang to mind "he catches pigeons."

He is of a small build around 5ft 7 inches tall. An out and out winger. A product of the Hull City academy who cost Swansea an initial fee of £72,000.

I recommended that we look at him as a potential emerging development target. It was revealed in January that he was all set to join Leeds United, but the deal fell through at the last minute. I firmly believed he would soon move to the Premiership and be a rising star. Well how about that? M********* United have bought him while I'm finalising this book. I hope this is one that I got wrong.

James has six International caps, with two goals coming in that time. I am sure more will follow in the coming years.

Watch him closely!

There have been players of course, that I have rejected or considered not up to scratch for one reason or another such as Raheem Sterling. I felt when he was at Liverpool, he wasted the final ball too often for my liking, often giving away possession and setting up an opposition counter attack in the process. I always remember what Arthur Cox told me, write what you see on the day, not what you think, or on reputation. We signed him and the rest is history. Pep has transformed him into the first name on the team sheet. I'm glad to have been proved wrong.

Riyad Mahrez was another one. When he was at Leicester, I felt he was inconsistent. He has taken time to settle in and I firmly believe we have not seen the best of him, but he needs time and then I am sure there is more to come from him. Pep will do the same to him as he has done with Raheem, I have no doubt.

There have been more that I could mention on all fronts. What I would say is that banking and football are similar, in that any scout that says he has not made a mistake on a player one way or another is not telling the truth.

It's like the Bank Manager that says he has never lost money lending it to a customer. Well, he has never lent any money to lose.

Over the years, I have met many great people like Mickey Walker, an ex-pro who also managed and was Director of football at Doncaster Rovers, we are good friends and speak regularly.

Dave Wright, a scout currently with Leicester City. He is a very knowledgeable, and well-respected scout on the circuit.

Glynn Snodin, a full back who played for Doncaster Rovers in 1977 before moving on to bigger things in 1985 and then joining Leeds United in 1987. He had a great career moving into coaching when he retired. We see each other from time to time on the circuit, we always share a laugh or two.

Ian Snodin is another. He played for Doncaster Rovers in midfield from 1980 before moving on to bigger and better things in 1985, when he was transferred to Leeds United and then moving again to Everton in 1987. I used to see him on my visits to Goodison (Everton F.C.) where he works as an ambassador.

David Fernandez, a wonderful character and one that every club needs. Before he came to City, he was an ex-pro at Celtic for a few seasons and spent much of his time in Scotland before and after that move. He and I got on and still get on very well to this day. A great guy! (See photo on page.................)

Also, people like Andy Hansen who have been scouting for over 40 years. Derek Bell, Tony Askew who were regulars on the scouting circuit.

I could name many, many more, but there are too many to mention.

Me and David Fernandez.

10

THE FINAL CHAPTER

Kevin Keegan

At this point, I feel it is a good time to say a few things about Kevin and put my slant on things that have been said about him walking away from jobs.

This could not be further from the truth, yes, he left clubs even as a player, but always left them on a better footing than when he joined.

As a player he told Liverpool that he was going to join Hamburg in Germany nearly 12 months in advance of leaving, they were still winning things like European Cups after he left. It gave Liverpool time to find a suitable replacement for him, although many said he could not be replaced. Liverpool signed a decent player in Kenny Dalglish. He has become a legend at Anfield. So, no harm done there then. He finished his career at Newcastle, deciding to leave when he felt it was time to hang up his boots as his legs were going and he no longer had that extra pace that made the difference.

Not many people know, but his contract or part of it was based on the attendances at St James' Park. He worked miracles and more than doubled the gate during his spell at Newcastle, so again no harm done, both parties benefited. Later Kevin revealed he was embarrassed by the whole thing and I seem to recall he gave them some money back. But in truth they had done well from him. He left the stadium after his final game with his family by helicopter, which landed on the pitch. Another team he left in a better position than when he joined.

Terry McDermott (Right), and son Paul with Kevin Keegan.

He had of course had success with Hamburg before returning to England and joining Southampton in 1980, managed by Lawrie McMenemy, ironically the last manager I worked for at Doncaster Rovers.

He took over as manager of Newcastle in 1992 and they won promotion to the Premiership as champions, maintained their Premier League status and finished 2nd to M********* United in season 1995/1996, having let what seemed an unassailable lead slip away. But again, look where he took them to.

I do remember just prior to Kevin selling Andy Cole to M********* United, we had been up to St James' Park to watch a game again, ironically against Manchester City, Kevin showed us around the very impressive stadium and made Steve Howie buy us a drink (winding him up). Paul, my son, was only 10 and insisted he wore his Liverpool shirt under his jumper, I gave Kevin and Terry McDermott the nod, so they started to tease him, Paul gave as good as he got saying that Bruce Grobbelaar had thrown the ball into the net in a recent match, Terry Mac said, "Ok, we can't really fault him given our background."

Lynda, Paul and I took up our seats in Kevin's private box along with his wife Jean and their two daughters Laura and Sarah, who were around the same age as Paul.

Newcastle won 3-1 with a ball playing (ahead of his time) centre back Phillipe Albert, bringing the ball out over the halfway line, before chipping the keeper. Kevin had told me sometime earlier that season that he would take the Premiership by storm - he was right.

After the game we went down to reception to wait for Kevin, the place was heaving, Phillippe Albert arrived and stood next to us at the reception desk waving a piece of paper. We overheard him ask the receptionist

"Where do I pick up my winnings, I backed myself to score and win 3-1."

Jean looked at me and I looked at her.

"Is he supposed to do that?" Jean asked.

"Well it's not illegal, but I don't think so." I replied.

"Don't tell Kevin." Jean said.

We kept quiet, Phillippe picked up his winnings, all was good.

Of course, you would not get away with that today, even I am barred from gambling on any football match worldwide.

My son Paul now aged 35, works for William Hill as a manager and has told me that following a letter from the FA, he had put me on a blacklist so I can't place a football based bet with them. (Saved me a lot of money!)

Anyway, back to Andy Cole, I phoned Kevin the same day as the sale went through having seen him on the steps outside reception, explaining why he had sold Andy Cole to United.

I told him "For what it is worth, I think it was the right decision", but I seemed to be in the minority.

"Why did you say that?" He asked.

My response was "I really thought he was Manchester City's best player on the day. He gave away possession cheaply, attacks broke down as a result of that and others seemed to be getting frustrated. He might be scoring goals, but I think he will get sussed with your team in due course.

He told me that I was spot on and that he and Terry Mac had sat down and counted on one hand the number of good games he had, taking away the goals. So, in many respects, I had an eye for scouting then but did not know it.

Kevin eventually departed Newcastle following a disagreement between him, the club and the club's bankers who I think were NatWest, about raising money from the sale of Les Ferdinand. Kevin thought the fans were being cheated and wanted no part of it.

He later returned to Newcastle but his relationship with Mike Ashley and others within the club were far from harmonious, so he resigned, again the club was in a much better position, but history shows he was right about the management structure when you look at the situation since and especially now.

He subsequently left Fulham and Manchester City on a much better footing than when he took over and always kept them informed as to why he was going to leave, especially the England job that he had turned down once before. He ended his spell as England Manager because he felt he could not do the job; he liked the day-to-day contact with players and with England and any other International team, he would not get that.

I remember watching the game against Germany at Wembley, which England lost 1-0 as he walked back down the tunnel, he paused and looked behind him towards the pitch. I said to Lynda, there's something wrong. Having known him for many years and he wears his heart on his sleeve I said he was going to resign. He left England for the good of the country and again, like everywhere else, without a payoff.

It transpired England's loss was Manchester City's gain. I have already outlined what happened and why he left, so whilst people can say I am biased and perhaps I am, but there is no denying that everywhere he has been he has left his mark and built a foundation for others to follow and develop. He has lost a fortune in payoffs, but he can hold his head high. It's not always about money, it's more than that, it's about integrity and doing what is right. In my mind, he has done that for the benefit of the teams he has been manager of and at some cost to himself.

The Women's Game

Whilst I do not propose to say I know anything about the onset of the rise and development in the Women's game, I do believe the fundamentals must surely be the same; in the respect of what you look for in a player or indeed what information, you need to prepare an opposition match report.

What I am aware of, is the fact that MCFC ladies share the same facilities as the senior men's team as well as the Academy players. This would never have been the case only a few years ago.

When I visit the training campus, you can see the lady players in and around the building, in and out of the restaurant and using the training facilities etc.

With the rise and development from teams such as Arsenal, Chelsea, and of course Manchester City. The investment in the lady's game has risen and I firmly believe will continue to rise, and see further growth in the domestic game, which will add to the increased interest at International level for England and other nations.

With the start of the Women's World Cup, the game had a great opportunity to launch itself to a new level with over 1 million tickets already sold for the competition. The opening game was sold out with over 48,000 expected. Speaking of the first game for our

Lionesses, as I finalise my book, they have just beaten Scotland 2-1 with a staggering 6.1 million people watching on TV, I suspect This World Cup could and after that first game, launch the women's game to an unprecedented level. I predict that will be the case leading to a very bright future ahead. Now is the perfect time to get involved in some way.

You only have to look at the victory parade that took place in Manchester, for the senior team who won four trophies including the Community Shield. The ladies had their own open top bus and shared the stage to celebrate their successes as well in the 2018/19 season. They finished 2nd in the Super League, topping that by winning both domestic cups; the FA Cup and the WSL Cup.

It occurred to me, this must open more doors for people to get involved. Perhaps even a lady, who does not make it as a professional player (no different to my experiences) could make a name for themselves and get involved as part of the background team.

I feel there are great opportunities ahead for anybody getting involved in the non-playing part of the ladies game and I hope that the forms, which outline the basic characteristics included as part of my information base used over the years, helps someone to say "I will give it a go."

I remember what my son once told me. If you don't ask the question, then the answer will always be NO.

Going back to the World Cup, I watched the tournament from my living room and was rather impressed with Christiane Endler of Chile. She is a number 1 and it is not difficult to see why she has been with Chelsea and now with PSG. I haven't seen many women's players, but she stood out and is the best I have seen.

Gibraltar Scousers

As mentioned, my son Paul works and lives in Gibraltar with his girlfriend Karla (a Scouser). He is in the gambling trade, as is Karla.

We make regular visits to them to enjoy the climate and their company, I always need a holiday when I get back! On such visits we meet up with many of their friends who are also employed in the gambling trade such as Emily and Sharon, two great girls.

Many of the people we meet are from Liverpool, the majority of whom support the red side of Liverpool with the occasional Blue (Phil). To say I have taken some stick and still do, especially over the last few years is an understatement (Steve and Danny in particular).

I have been there when we played Liverpool and won convincingly and had to quieten the crowd of Reds, being the only Manchester City man in the room with the banter in full flow, but I took them on. Someone asked Paul, "Is that your Dad?" Paul replied yes to which the guy replied, "That's great for standing up and being counted and for not being quiet in a room full of reds."

More recently with Liverpool on the ascendancy, the banter between us has increased in its intensity and volume. We were there recently when MCFC played Everton and again the volume was turned up with the Reds taunting me that we were 8 points behind before playing Everton later in the day, although Phil (the blue) said he was supporting MCFC if only to help stop Liverpool from winning the league, he said he could not bear it. I had a supportive colleague in the Ivy bar. Especially as earlier in the day when Liverpool had beaten Sheffield United 1-0 away at Bramall Lane, with a lucky goal, following a mistake from the United keeper.

It only registered to me how many Liverpool supporters were in the bar when Liverpool scored and around 40 to 50 people started jumping up and down delirious with joy, especially Danny and Steve, boy did I get some stick.

With the Reds singing at the top of their voices "we are top of the league (repeated time after time) I had to wait my time until the chant subsided. I jumped into the Lions Den and started singing at the top of my voice (Not for long not for long…………..) I was now getting more stick than ever, but as always with these guys it's friendly banter and respect is guaranteed between us, as we both like to see United lose and come together knowing we are the best two teams in the league by a country mile.

It did not end there, later in the day at 17.30, we were back in the Ivy, this time to watch Manchester City away at Everton.

I was again walking into the lions den again, well imagine the stick I was getting. We were 8 points behind and struggling against a dogged Everton, who were not rolling over or lying down as Steve kept telling me they would. We had a game on our hands.

Danny kept taunting me saying "you must be getting worried now." (Which I was, we could not afford to drop more points.)

With 71 mins gone we were still level at 1-1 then Mahrez struck with a terrific free kick to put us 1-2 up, I jumped up in celebration, the room went a little quiet as I shouted "do you want Var again?" The banter intensified. Finally, we sealed the game with an 84th minute goal by Sterling.

They still chanted "we are top of the league" I came back again with "not for long, not for long….."

I said to Danny, "you were 8 points ahead last year", he quickly replied, "No, 7 points!"

Until now, I have escaped unscathed from the lions den with support from my minder and fellow blue Phil, albeit a different blue.

But I await the day, even though I have retired from MCFC, that we slip up and Liverpool beat us with me in a bar in Gibraltar, surrounded by passionate Scousers, can you believe the stick and banter I will get?

Finally, I am sure I have missed people out, so very sorry, but the number of people in all honesty who come up and say, "Are you Starrzy's Mum and Dad?"

They make us feel so welcome. It's unbelievable and I have lost count the number of drinks I have turned down. I shall say no more otherwise I would be permanently drunk.

There is one name we met in Bruno's whom I must mention. That is Harry. What a character! I will say no more.

One thing is for sure, they all work hard and that includes the ladies, but they play even harder.

God bless you all for your hospitality when we visit Gibraltar, but I will be carefully selecting our next visit in line with the Premier league fixtures, you see, I am not that stupid to walk into the lions den without the value bet in my favour.

How lucky have I been?

Putting this together is something I have considered for some time. However, I did not think it would generate as many pages as it has. I would like to thank Pierre Quinquenel a man I had never heard of, never even met before, he is an ex-NatWest player, who played for the bank after I'd left London, for asking me to write the memories down. I will be able to refer to them when I am no longer in a position to go scouting anymore.

It has brought back memories and things that I had forgotten over the years. It has reminded me that at the age of nine, I won my first medal as a player, playing for Edington Victoria Road School situated around 50 yards from where I was married to Lynda on the 6th September 1975. However, having played in every game up to the final, my Grandfather whom I was very close to, living in a place called Twechar near Glasgow, died in the week leading up to the final, so I missed the final as we had to go to Scotland for his funeral.

It also brought it home to me that at the age of 66 I was winning a Premiership title and League Cup as a senior scout with Manchester City. A period of 57 years apart and still counting. In between, there have been many successes, and I am proud to say that I have never been involved as a player, a manager or a scout with a team that has been relegated.

I have worked for some great managers since I started scouting Kevin Keegan (twice), Paul Bracewell, Jean Tigana, Stuart Pearce, Mark Hughes, Sven Goran Eriksson, Roberto Mancini, Manuel Pellegrini, and currently Pep Guardiola; who is bringing football for Manchester City to a new level.

I have said again in my story "how lucky have I been?!"

On that subject, I was saying the very same thing to a fellow scout and whilst luck will always play its part, to be involved at so many levels including reaching Regional Manager status with NatWest, life needs more than just luck.

He said, "I know you very well and it's amazing the harder you've worked, the luckier you've become" - Food for thought.

I do maintain that it's better to have the 'it's who you know', not 'what you know' to give you that start. Putting this down on paper brought it home. I have made some life changing decisions which have helped along the way, none more so than going to the hospital, as opposed to going to work. There are too many others to mention, but I look back on them and say to myself, "yes, that decision paid off!"

Put them all together and you have a process that points you in the right direction.

I would like to say to a few people, thank you for their support in recent years. As time has moved on my health has not been as good, although now quite stable if not sometimes quite complicated with the brain tumour and the onset of Parkinson's. Not to mention the other ailments!

My immediate line manager, Alan Watson, scouting and recruitment manager UK and Gavin Fleig, head of global strategy lead talent management, have seamlessly reduced my workload although, they will probably deny it, but I have noticed. The last 10 years have been a rocket ship rise to the top and it's still climbing. I was there from the start and played my part. They now look after me and I don't cover as much, but they have made sure I still have an important part to play across the whole City Football Group and use me accordingly.

Alan is very considerate in what he gives me to maximise my time, at the most recent global conference I had a chat with Gavin Fleig, who asked how I was. I said "ok, not as clever as I once was, but if I thought I could not do the job anymore I would call it a day."

Gavin came straight back at me and I will summarize his response.

He started to mention that I had done my bit over the last 18 years or so and seen the club develop to where it is today, I still have an important role to play in assessing players and that the word quickly goes around the scouting and recruitment office, if I give a player a rating of 'B' or God forbid an 'A'.

At a previous conference, Gavin awarded a prize for the scout with the most consistent record in player reports.

"And the winner is… John Starrs with an amazing 98%", at which point from under the table he pulled a mug with a giant 'D' engraved on the mug!

"On most of his reports he gives a 'D', everybody laughed including me, but then Gavin added the above comment about what happens when I give a 'B' or an 'A'.

Second from the left, front row!

He then went on to say I owe this club nothing, they owe you, if you need us to change things then we will change things - because you are going nowhere.

I was choked but delighted to hear his words, he made me feel ten feet tall and wanted. Normally in football it's not like that.

That being said, Manchester City are no ordinary club, with no ordinary people such as Alan and Gavin, James Smith and Fergal Harkin, plus others I have not mentioned.

I make no apologies for stating the obvious about luck but, who you know, hard work and decision making all played its part in me being lucky.

Trophy delight

HERE'S a belting sporting image from the sixties.

A wonderfully well thumbed photograph of the Victoria Junior Boys Soccer Team at Edlington who were winners of the Gundry Shield in 1962 and my word they look proud too.

Those smiles tell us just how proud these lads are and rightly so. But where does the name Gundry come from and who are these super soccer champs? Some readers out there will know exactly so off we go down memory lane once again starting with that all important name check

Top, left to right.

Mark Hepplestone, Martin Henry (who sent in the picture).

Derek Wardle, John Jolley, John Glover, Arthur Woods (deceased), Dave McEwan, Denis Phillips, Lester Ainsworth,

Billy Shillyto, John Starr, Billy Hodgson, David Wakelin and Fred Watson.

Fifty years in a drawer, being passed from hand to hand and studied by eager young fingers the picture has definitely seen better days but the occasion and the look of triumph is priceless.

I left that conference with a spring in my step, full of confidence that I was still wanted and had a part to play in the future growth of Manchester City and City Football Group.

What I would like to do is dedicate the contents to the following people.

Bernard Halford, a life president of Manchester City who sadly passed away earlier this year at the age of 77. He was City through and through, RIP.

The late Willie O'Donnell, who served Manchester City for over 45 years before his sudden passing a few years ago.

To John Ferguson, who is still scouting and will be nearing 50 years with Manchester City a record that will, in my opinion, never be surpassed.

They are, and have been, wonderful ambassadors for Manchester City going through the bad times and in the last ten years, been part of the club's best time ever. They all kept their enthusiasm every time I met up with them.

In my career, as part of Fulham and Manchester City's scouting and recruitment staff for both clubs over a 21-year period, I have been part of the following winning trophy successes.

	Manchester City	Fulham
Premier League	4	
FA Cup	2	
League Cup	4	
Community Sheild	2	
Championship	1	1
League	1	1
Total	13	2
	15	

To achieve 15 trophies spanning a 21-year involvement in football is remarkable. I have said before many scouts go through their careers and win nothing.

I have had two wonderful careers in banking and in professional football scouting. I count myself very lucky.

I would like to add that the club will miss Vincent Kompany, he is a legend now that he has decided to leave for pastures new and a different challenge. Thanks to his leadership and his devotion, he is without doubt a gentleman. Best wishes to him and I have a sneaky suspicion he will not be the only one leaving the club before the new season starts. You never know!

Writing these memoirs has made me reflect on my time in football both as a player and for last 21 years as a scout.

Initially, I have said I took the fact that I did not make it as a player very hard, in fact it was a burden on my shoulders for many years.

I even refused to take my son Paul to watch Lincoln City for many years, because I could not watch players whom I felt were very average and from what I was watching, were no better than I was in my younger days. I regret that decision to this day as I punished my son for my misgivings.

However, when I look how many young boys grow up wanting to be footballers but only a few are chosen. When you look at Manchester City for example, they have a first team squad of 25-30 players, but look how many youngsters that come through the ranks ever break into that squad. Currently at Manchester City, Phil Foden is the only one.

Many will go on to play for other clubs and some will drift in and out of clubs. In fact, many when you look on a larger scale, will drop and fade out of football altogether without achieving a career.

These days, there are many opportunities in football other than playing which is the holy grail, but like me I have found a way to be involved in some way.

For example, there is the scouting route that I took on at various levels, there is the medical side, nutritionists. A player can't just have a burger when they feel like it, they are monitored very closely.

There has been a large increase in technology that has seen the growth in analysts, some don't even need to see the game live, they can watch the game on a screen as if you are there.

On this point, I believe the life of the scout as it used to be will fade. We are dying breed, being taken over by analysts and technology. I often see analysts at games using iPad's to record situations such as set pieces transition play etc. I believe there is a place for both to run side by side, but I fear this will not be the case. Technology will prevail and overtake the old-fashioned scout in the near future, which will see their demise.

What it does show though, is the growth in resources at a team like Manchester City. Nowadays, to be successful, you have to do the hard work off the pitch, to give the guys on the pitch, the best chance of winning. This opens doors for many people like me who have been rejected by a club and still want to carve out a career in the football industry. This wasn't available when I was rejected, so it can only be a good thing it's there now, as it took me a long time to shed the burden, I was carrying on my back by not making it as a player.

Analysts nowadays do most of their research and reports from behind a desk. When I was going to watch a player or do an opposition match report abroad for example, I would get up very early around 2am to drive to an airport so I could check in for my flight to say Poland, Serbia, Romania. After the flight, I would arrive at my destination, get to the stadium only to find out the player I was supposed to be watching was not even on the bench sometimes, never mind actually playing.

The same happened to me in the UK. On occasions, the player I was going to watch would not play. That is very frustrating having taken longer to get to the game than the game itself. I would stay though, because the club has got tickets reserved for me and it would be rude not to stay. In any case, there could be a young player starting that I could cover, this did happen from time to time. On the other hand, there were so many times it was a wasted journey. Scouting on the whole though, especially for players, is extremely frustrating in that nothing comes from your efforts. You live by the occasions where it all comes together, which makes it worthwhile. You learn to handle the frustrations as the years roll on.

When I think about it, at its peak I was probably covering around 120 games a season travelling the length and breadth of the country as far south as Bournemouth and Southampton up to Glasgow in Scotland. When you live in Lincoln, wherever I go is not a short journey as I'm least 40 minutes from the A1 and an hour from the M1.

People often ask me what I regard as my best moment in Football overall. They think I am going to say the time Manchester City won the first Premiership title, as I was involved with many of the reports that season including the three against M********* United. They may also think it's from my time at Fulham, or indeed the fact that I have been at City for over 19 years and I feel I am there on merit.

But they would all be wrong…

My most pleasing, most satisfying moment came after I had retired at the age of 38/39, playing in a friendly for Branston FC in Lincoln where I was manager along with Richard Kwiatkowski, a good friend of mine, against RAF Waddington.

My son Paul who was aged about nine at the time and Lynda came to watch. We won the game, I had a game that I will never forget, Paul recalled it to me, he remembered that I scored the perfect hat-trick (a header, a right foot shot (very rare for me) and finally, an overhead kick with my left foot).

But it was when I was leaving the pitch at the end of the game, Paul came running on straight towards me and said,

"Dad that was great, you must have been some player in your day." That meant so much to me and still does, writing these memoirs brought it all back, and the fact that he remembers it to this day makes it more special.

Well I've done it, I've written my stories down.

I hope you enjoyed reading them!